JEMEZ MOUNTAINS 100 YEARS AGO

Stories told by Joseph E. Routledge

Edited by Judith Ann Isaacs

Butterfly & Bear Press
995 Vista Hermosa Rd.
Jemez Pueblo, NM 87024

ISBN 978-0-9629645-5-8

Cover photo*: Art, Ethel, Herb, Joe, Dorothy & Bettie Routledge in buckboard with horses, Dolly & Star, 1925.*
Title page photo: *Routledge family at Freelove Canyon house, 1928.*
All photos provided by Robert Borden and used with permission.

◄►TABLE OF CONTENTS◄►

Introduction i

Acknowledgments ii

Map.. iii

JEMEZ PLACES

Jemez Tour as I Best Remember 2
Freelove Canyon 4
Cattle Brands 7
Thompson Ridge 7
Jemez Mountains Churches 10
Springs of the Jemez 12
Healing Waters at Sulphur Springs 14
Minerals of the Jemez Mountains 17
Voting in the Old Days 19
Voting in the Old Days: Part 2 20
Jemez Indian Irrigation 21
The Fish Plant 22
My Trip to Town in 1928 25
Long Look Back at La Cueva 28

RANCH LIFE

Country Kids 32
Backhouses 33
We Reset the Outhouse 35
Mama's Piano 36
Lost Child 40
Wild Mushrooms 42
Del Monte Peas 44
Meat and Potatoes Diet 45
When Lightning Walked About 47

A Lot of Bad Luck 49
When Someone Passes Away 51

ANIMAL ADVENTURES
A Hunter Wrestles a Deer 54
A Sticky Porcupine 55
Horses Can See in the Dark 57
Skunks 59
Chicken Thief 61
Jemez Springs Turkeys 62
Mad Dog Scare of 1928 64
A Deer Named Daisy 66
Dolly's Family 68
Last Wolf in the Jemez 70
Pet the Cow 72
Jemez Mountains Mustangs 74
Mike's Bear 75
Mike the Trapper................................ 78
Saga of Montrose the Cow 79
Horses in the Big Log Woods 81

MOUNTAIN TRAVEL
Blazing Trails 84
Bridges of Sandoval County 85
Rough Road to Jemez Gets Paved 87
When We Traded Wagons for Cars 89
Water for Our Radiators 91
When Railroads Came to the Jemez 93
A Ride on a Baldey Truck 95

MOUNTAIN FOLK
A Can of Sardines 99
The Wild Man of New Mexico 100
John Barleycorn 102

The Bee Man 103
Hey, Water Boy! 105
Gun Fight at Bland 106
The Man Who Trained Burros 108
Rancho Rea: A Hideaway for the Wanted 110
Sheep Camp 112
Some Trout Fish 114
The Jemez Bell 116
Lost on the Baca Ranch 118

About the Storyteller & Editor 121

◄►INTRODUCTION ◄►

From 1999 to 2002, a small community newspaper in northern New Mexico published a series of stories about life in the Jemez Mountains 100 years ago. At that time, this part of New Mexico was like living on the frontier; life was fraught with hardship and danger.

Joseph (Joe) Elmer Routledge was an infant in 1920 when his father brought his wife and two young sons to an abandoned ranch northeast of the Village of Jemez Springs. Although the ranch was a mere 12 miles from the Village, there was no road to speak of, and the trip took all day in a wagon. An indefatigable entrepreneur, Art Routledge supported his family by—to name a few of his endeavors—trading and training horses, running cattle on the open range, supplying lumber camps, growing potatoes, and renting cabins (which he built) to tourists at the sulphur springs.

Despite what many today would consider a rough upbringing, Joe Routledge, who died in 2014, wrote about his childhood with nostalgia and humor. His correspondence with Kathleen Wiegner and Robert Borden, owners and publishers of the *Jemez Thunder,* reveals that they had intended to publish a book of these stories. However, this never came to pass. In 2020, Robert Borden published the last *Jemez Thunder*, retired, moved from Jemez Springs, and gave his blessing to this book project.

Sixty of the 67 stories Joe wrote are included. I have edited as little as possible in order to keep the vocabulary and syntax of the original stories and to avoid repetition. Most of the titlesare those written at the time of first publication in the *Jemez Thunder*. Any mistakes or interpretations are entirely my own.

◄►ACKNOWLEDGMENTS◄►

I would like to thank Robert Borden for making at least a half dozen trips in his Mini Cooper to deposit all Routledge memorabilia, as well as all back issues of the *Jemez Thunder*, under my portal.

My thanks to Theodore Greer, Erma Ruth, Irene Wanner, and Nancy Koven for reading the manuscript and providing feedback. Also thanks to Erica Kane for the map and cover design.

Judith Isaacs
Sandoval County, New Mexico
2020

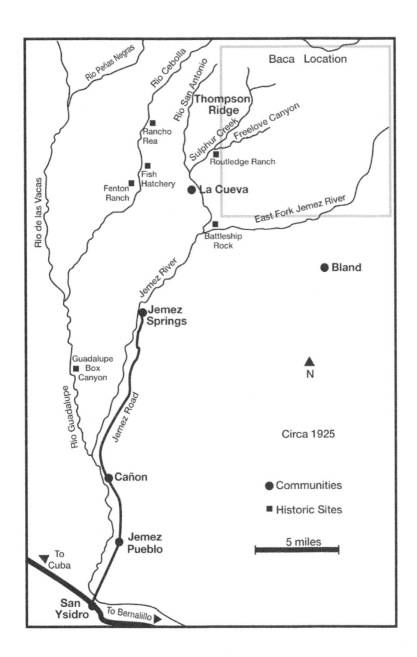

Baca Location

Rio Peñas Negras
Rio Cebolla
Rio San Antonio
Rio de las Vacas

Thompson
Ridge

Rancho
Rea

Sulphur Creek
Freelove Canyon

Routledge Ranch

Fish
Hatchery

Fenton
Ranch

La Cueva

East Fork Jemez River

Battleship
Rock

Jemez River

Bland

Jemez
Springs

Guadalupe
Box
Canyon

N

Rio Guadalupe

Jemez Road

Circa 1925

Cañon

Communities

Historic Sites

Jemez
Pueblo

5 miles

To
Cuba

San
Ysidro

To Bernalillo

iii

JEMEZ PLACES

Routledge Ranch
1941

◄►JEMEZ TOUR AS I BEST REMEMBER◄►

The best way to tell of the people that lived in the Jemez Valley in the 1920s is to start at Cañon. There were several houses near the school and more across the river where the Gilman road turns off. There were a number of farms up the (Spanish-speaking) Guadalupe on the west side of Jemez Canyon from here.

There were adobe buildings on the west side of the road to Jemez Springs, and the Burnett copper mine, which operated until about 1938, was on the right side. *[Ed. Note: This mine was later known as the Spanish Queen.]* Then only a couple of little ranchitos until closer to Jemez Springs. Near Jemez Springs was a cluster of houses and a dance hall owned by Tony Maestas, where fiestas and dances were held frequently. Tony played the fiddle, and volunteers came with guitars and concertinas or mouth harps. This was country music, and all the young people learned to dance. This cluster of houses was occupied by Spanish-speaking families and was cruelly named "goat town." Then there was a gap of no houses, except that of the Abousleman alfalfa fields and barns between the road and the river.

About the first house on the left in Jemez Springs belonged to the Fluke family, and they ran the telephone exchange. The next place on the left was the school. *[Ed. Note: Jemez Mountains Electric Cooperative stands on this site now.]* On the right was the J. D. Johnston store. Again on the left (where the post office was built in later years) was a little adobe house occupied by "Doc" Holloway, whom we called Doc Hollow-leg, as he had a wooden leg due to a train accident years before. He had been a medical doctor but was unlicensed, but he was all we had for first aid and to set broken bones, etc.

Across the road to the right was the Block Hotel and its spread of cabins and apartments. The post office was here, and was run by a Mr. Woodgate and his wife. She had an aviary, and it was the first time we had ever seen a canary. About 1924, part of Block's Hotel burned on what I think is the piece of land where the American Legion hall is now. *[Ed. Note: The social hall for the Catholic Church stands on this site now.]* Next on the right was the Union Hall. Across the street to the left was Billy Mann's store and gasoline pump. Here was the post office for some years. Next on the left side was the nice Abousleman house where Moses and his family lived. In later years there was a gas station and store owned by Mrs. Beard. Across the street was the Presbyterian Church where Rev. Berry was minister for 50 years. Next was Los Ojos bar, owned by the Abousleman brothers, and it had a gun collection on the walls that was the best in New Mexico. There was a huge hay barn next door north. Across the road west was open ground with the bathhouses—they were wooden and had a wooden walkway all around them.

Further up the canyon was a small house on the right occupied by Mr. White and his family. Next on the left was Mr. Wroth's place. Now we are at the old church. *[Ed. Note: This is now the Jemez Historic Site.]* Across the road was Mrs. Miller's place. She and her son, Hugh, had an extensive orchard and garden. Hugh was an expert grafter of trees and bushes, and produced fruit and vegetables rivaling California's. This place was sold to someone about 1936, and a dinner house and hotel was built. The Catholic Church bought this up after it failed, and became Via Coeli, now the Servants of the Paraclete. The church bought and still holds a lot of land down the Jemez canyon.

North of Soda Dam were signs of old bathhouses near the springs. From here to Battleship Rock, there were several farms on the river including Hummingbird Lodge and the fabulous Rancho Chico that Seth Seiders built for his wife at the time Rancho Rea was built on the Cebolla (Lazy Ray Ranch).

Howard Roland's place was the last up the canyon and the end of where fruit would grow. Battleship Rock, even then, was a favorite place for people to camp and pitch their tents on vacation. The fishing was good, and it was a beautiful spot!

Jemez Springs can be viewed from the west rim above and there is a good trail to hike up to the top, built by the retired padres at Via Coeli. You will see it is quite a small village when you count the roofs!

This story appeared in the Jemez Thunder, *June 15, 1999.*

◄►FREELOVE CANYON◄►

Where Freelove Creek and Sulphur Creek come together, the little meadow was homesteaded by a Mr. Freelove. The homestead covered 88 acres and extended along both creeks. There were huge yellow pine trees growing here, so Mr. Freelove brought in a little steam sawmill and turned these trees into rough-cut lumber. He built a good hay barn and other buildings, such as a milk barn, tool sheds, chicken house, calf pens and a large corral, which was made out of slabs from the mill, high and strong. He also made a smaller round corral with a snubbing post in the center for branding and handling the bronco horses.

He leveled a one-acre garden spot in the best soil and put a picket fence around it. He cleared 40 acres down the canyon for oat-hay and five small fields for potatoes and barley. All of this he enclosed with a good barbed wire fence and divided some forest land into a horse pasture, calf pasture and cow pasture. Each pasture had water in them, and he diverted water to the garden for irrigation and through the corrals so the livestock could always have water. He dug a root cellar into the hillside which had hollow walls and a roof which he insulated with two feet of sawdust from the mill. Potatoes and root vegetables could be kept all season without freezing or spoiling.

Mr. Freelove then built his house, which was the only two-story north of Jemez Springs. It had three bedrooms upstairs and a nice staircase down to a parlor, a dining room, kitchen, two bedrooms and a small room for guns and storage for supplies. On the north side—the coolest and shadiest part of the house—there was a small room to keep milk and perishable things. There was a full-length covered porch on the south side of the house, and a back porch. The subfloor was made of two-inch slabs and covered with tongue and groove pine. The inside walls were smooth and covered with nice wallpaper. The outside walls were ship-lap, and the hollow walls were filled with sawdust from the mill. All the work was careful and precise. Only the foundation was not so great, as it was big selected rocks and no cement.

There was a cold spring nearby that never went dry. There was a woodshed at the back door and an outhouse beyond that, with clotheslines between the two. The house was painted green with white trim. The house was built on a hill so that one could survey the corrals and the fields away from the flies and safe from flood.

It was a fine homestead. The story goes that he built for a certain lady who he finally brought to see his work. She stayed only one day after the brutal trip into the wilderness and declared that she could never live here. She left at once.

Poor Mr. Freelove was heartbroken, and he soon left his place. He stopped in Jemez Springs and sold it to a Mr. Block for a pittance. It was just after World War I, and no one had any money. It was abandoned for a while. In 1920, my dad came along with a reputation as a go-getter, and Mr. Block let him in for $25 down and $25 per month, which everyone doubted he could make.

We had a hard time trying to pay for it, but wild horses, potatoes and cows let us get title. It became the Routledge place, and we called it the Bar Heart, which was our registered brand. My sister Dorothy still holds the brand. We were comfortable here, although we never had any power, running water or gas heat. We built the place up with 12 summer cabins for the tourist trade and had some cattle and horses and bought Thompson Ridge.

In 1942, while we were all away at war, my dad had a heart attack and died. All the ranch holdings were sold, and an Italian businessman became the owner of the home place. It was never operated as a ranch again. It wound up in the possession of an out-of-state owner and later someone's estate. It was abandoned for many years, and the hippies used it for shelter. The house burned down about 1970.

Now houses are being built in our potato fields, and the ranch is alive again.

This story appeared in the Jemez Thunder, *July 1, 2000.*

◄►CATTLE BRANDS◄►

Nearly all of the people who owned cattle had their own brand. There were only a few ranchers in the Jemez Mountains who had cattle, and most of them were scattered a long ride away! The largest owners were on the Baca Location, and their cattle were surrounded in an area with a 12x12 fence that covered 144 square miles of the Valles Caldera. They all had their own brands, and we only saw their cattle when they would wander up against our ranch fences. They were kept on their own ranges by the hard-riding cowboys that tended the fences and took care of the strays.

Our brand was called a Bar Heart—a heart with a bar through the middle. On the horses, the neat little brand was on the right hip. For the cows, it was on the right front shoulder. There was a nick in the right ear of the cows that were branded, as a backup in case any brand was altered.

Our closest neighbor was Angus Fetterson's mother, and she had about 30 or 40 cows on Thompson Ridge where she lived in a log cabin on the homestead. *[Editor's note: More about Mrs. Fetterson in the next story.]*

My sister Dorothy still has the Bar Heart brand, and it is registered to her. She lives in Roswell and has only two horses. She married Alex Hill, one of the cowboys from the Baca Ranch.

This story appeared in the Jemez Thunder, *April 15, 2002.*

◄►THOMPSON RIDGE◄►

The nice homes on Thompson Ridge are built on what was once a homestead. It was called Prairie Place, which we think was homesteaded by Fred Prairie. It was the highest, loneliest and most isolated of all the mountain ranches. It had a good log cabin with a stone fireplace and chimney and a small barn and some corrals. It had a fenced field of some 20 or 30 acres. No one seemed to live there, except in the early '20s it was occupied by a tough old gal of the Calamity Jane type.

She wore men's clothes, a slouch hat along with chaps and a big hog-leg six-shooter and always had a chaw of plug tobacco in her jaw. She was a scary one to meet on horseback. She had about 30 head of mangy cattle with long scary horns. She was called Grandma Fetterson. We shared the range where she ran her cattle. They were sometimes mixed with ours, and my brother and I dreaded having to separate them for fear of running into this spooky old woman. She would cuss at us and threaten to shoot us. She knew our dad quite well, and they sometimes talked trade for cows and horses, punctuated by a stream of profanity.

We don't know what arrangement she had to live in the cabin, but one day it burned down and she swore she would kill whoever burned her out. We thought it was a spark from the fireplace, but we never found out.

Angus, her son, had a 1911 .45 automatic, and he gave it to her as a Christmas present. She loved it because if she got into a fire fight, she would have nine rounds instead of six. Angus's stud, which he called Spike, got away from his barn in La Cueva and showed up with Grandma's horses. The first time she tried to use her new pistol was to try and kill old Spike. She got the automatic going and couldn't stop it, and the horse she was riding threw her. She lay on the ground for five days before someone came along to help her.

A broken hip was the end in those days, and she lay in the Block Hotel for several years. She sent for my dad and, after much bickering and cussing, he bought her herd, brand and all. She used the brand ZZZ and told my dad it was a bargain because a big herd at a nearby range used the brand 77, and it was an easy conversion. My dad decided not to do that and declined the idea.

No one ever lived at the Prairie Place again, but we used it to hold cattle for branding and sorting out the livestock. Glen Barber planted the field one year in potatoes but had to pack out the spuds on horses. This was a place where the trails from Sulphur Springs and the Valle Grande met to catch the trail to our place and La Cueva, or west over the mountain to Fentons. There were two small ponds nearby. We used to see riders traveling through.

In the 1930s, the place was purchased by a Mr. Thompson, who also owned the Lazy Ray dude ranch above the Seven Springs Fish Hatchery. Mr. Thompson was involved in a love triangle in Albuquerque, and when he threatened to beat up the woman's husband at his own house, the man promptly shot him dead as Thompson came down the walk. He was acquitted in court.

The little ranch was by now called the Thompson Place. When it went into an estate, we were able to buy it—much to our surprise and joy. The place had no road, but it was only about two miles by a good horse trail from our front gate. Just before World War II, New Mexico Lumber and Timber Company built the log road we now use. When the whole area was logged off, it was called Thompson Ridge.

My father died in 1942 and both ranches went into an estate. We were all away at war so my sister Dorothy, with some help from Steve Edsell, sold the livestock and the household goods. The two-story house at the home ranch at Freelove burned in 1970.

This story appeared in the Jemez Thunder, *September 1, 2000.*

◄►JEMEZ MOUNTAINS CHURCHES ◄►

Jemez Springs had only two churches to offer, but they took us through thick and thin. There was the Catholic Church and the Presbyterian. Most of the people in Jemez Springs were Catholic, but the little churches served our joys and griefs for many years and still remain side by side in Jemez Springs today.

Most of the far-out ranches were unchurched. When we got our first car, we could drive to Jemez Springs after an early morning breakfast, attend church, and get the mail. Before the time of automobiles, my mother had home-schooled us. On Sunday, she dressed us up, and we had Sunday school. We had a piano, so we learned the hymns and the Bible stories. I remember when we got our car, we went to hear Rev. Berry preach, and we improved his congregation by six people. Not only that, my mother played the piano, and we four children stood and sang "Onward, Christian Soldiers."

We were Presbyterians, and visited the church when we were only a few people to hear his sermon, and sometimes there were none, but he preached every Sunday. Of course, there was no money, and in the beginning Rev. Berry lived in a tent in back of the church, but eventually moved into an addition. Those of us who lived in La Cueva only came as we could.

The Hofheinses, both Tim and Attia, were Catholic; the Fentons and ourselves were Presbyterians.

Our neighbors, Tim and Attia, had children about the same age as we were: Harold was my age, and Ralph a little younger, and the baby girl, Leatha, was the youngest. One summer, the little girl became very ill and they thought she had eaten some "bear berries" that are very poisonous. She cried for days, and Tim borrowed our Ford and started for Albuquerque. At Jemez Springs she was about gone, and there was no doctor there, so the Hofheinses stopped at the Catholic Church and Father Louie came out and gave her the last rites. She died in her father's arms. (She died of appendicitis.) We were saddened by the loss of this child and realized how vulnerable we were without a doctor.

While we were away at World War II, my father had a heart attack as he was returning from a trip to Albuquerque in 1942. He was disabled in Bernalillo and Glen Barber drove him and his pickup to the ranch, and Louise followed in their truck. Art thought he would be well by morning. During the night and early morning hours, a couple of feet of snow fell, and my dad passed away. Glen was able to get to the highway and go to work. Buddy was sent to the Barbers for help, but nothing could be done.

As Glen came home from work, he knew the first thing he must do was to bring a coroner from Jemez Springs. The coroner found nothing wrong, so they wrapped him in a canvas tarp and put him in the back of Glen's pickup, and Louise tended the stock while Glen was gone. Then they had a couple of hours of shoveling snow to reach Highway 4. When they reached Jemez Springs, here was the good Rev. Berry with a crew, and was burning old tires to dig a hole in the frozen ground in the graveyard. They were told to hold on, and in Albuquerque the burial was delayed while all the relatives arrived. His mother and two sisters came from Phoenix and El Paso, along with all his children. He was buried in Fairview Cemetery in Albuquerque, and Rev. Berry consoled us all!

This story appeared in the Jemez Thunder, *December 15, 1999.*

◀▶SPRINGS OF THE JEMEZ◀▶

The mountains of the Jemez have always had a great many springs. Some hot and some cold, but never indifferent. Beginning at San Ysidro and looking north, there was a hot springs on the Cuba road, just beyond San Ysidro. That was an open air thing of soft warm water, used by a lot of the local people and those up toward La Ventana and Cuba.

The next big spring was at Jemez Springs where the swells (dudes with money) came to "take the waters." I had an Aunt Edna who taught at the first Cañon school in 1889, where in the beginning no one knew their ABCs and few spoke English. Aunt Edna wrote that Jemez Springs had a stagecoach that stopped there at a big bathhouse, with walkways and a place to sip the water. Mr. Block built the Block Hotel across the roadway, and the post office was in his house. Even after good autos could reach the Jemez in a single day, the trade fell off and never did well after World War I (1918).

There were springs above the Soda Dam that had really formed a dam across the Jemez River and canyon, during hundreds of years of soda deposits. We think there was a great flood, and the river washed out around the right side of the dam and now appears to flow through it. In our day, there were two open pits 50 yards above the dam, where you could bathe al fresco in the tepid water. There were signs of old bathhouses there.

The next one was Spence Hot Spring, one of the best and most used in the mountains. My dad was a special friend of Mr. Spence, who spent all his time at the hot spring. He tried so very hard to make it his. He applied for mining rights and squatters rights and even tried to buy the spring, all of which were denied by the Forest Service. He built a bridge across the river and a trail to the springs. He even built a crude bathhouse of peeled poles for privacy.

Poor Mr. Spence suffered ill health and finally gave up. The bridge washed out, and the Forest Service tore the hut down. So we crossed the river on a huge yellow pine log or stepping stones. The campground is still there, and signs of the old wagon road can be found. There is a smaller and hotter spring above and down a little way from Spence, but you can't bathe in it.

The next hot spring is on the San Antonio River above La Cueva. It is inside the Baca fence and is the biggest of all. It could fill a two-inch pipe day and night. Nice hot soft water, and it was our favorite. It took all day to go there and back on horses by way of Thompson Ridge. We bathed there and washed our clothes in its large pool. At my last look, it was fenced and posted private property. It was the best.

The next hot spring was Sulphur Springs, a mile and a half above Freelove Canyon and our ranch. It deserves a column by itself because of its great curative power and history. They are inside the Baca fence and is private property—40 acres. There are several sulphur springs on the Baca Ranch.

The people that settled the Jemez Mountains always built near a cold spring, or at least near a creek or river. There are dozens of good, cold, sweet springs all over the mountains, many never seen except by the cowboys and the hunters and loggers that travel away from the roads. A good example is the ice cold spring that spurts off the hillside into the road just a little way below the junction of Highways 4 and 126. There is a little spring on each side the steep old road over Fenton Hill, where we used to water our sweating team, and later, the steaming radiators of our old Fords. The Fenton Ranch had the coldest spring anywhere, about 36 degrees and a heavy flow.

All of us drank this water for 80 years or more and suffered no ill effects, despite the presence of arsenic, they say.

This story appeared in the Jemez Thunder, *October 1, 2000.*

◄► HEALING WATERS AT SULPHUR SPRINGS ◄►

Sulphur Springs has a long history, and its main forte has been its curative powers. The early settlers knew about it, and some said the Indians and the Spanish knew that the lightly-mixed sulphuric acid and warm water could cure almost any infection. The Sulphur Springs property is located inside the Baca Location, about a mile and a half above Freelove Canyon. It has always been considered private property with access guaranteed by the various owners of the Baca Land Grant, which was once owned by the famous Otero family.

Oteros built a smelter here to retrieve sulphur for the commercial market. The road out was so rough and long—in addition to the fact that the miners could not work in the heat and fumes once they started a tunnel— that the mill was abandoned. About the turn of the century, a three-story log hotel was built, along with several bathhouses, to cure the ailing people that came there. There was a stagecoach that came from Española via Los Alamos and the Valle Grande and entered Sulphur Springs from the north. The road to Jemez Springs was not used much. In 1925, a road crew came and made it so a good car could reach Sulphur Springs. The place began to boom, and was filled each summer.

Since our ranch at Freelove Canyon was the nearest ranch, we were able to supply the hotel with meat, milk, butter, cheese and eggs. We also had horses to rent and often brought mail and groceries and stranded dudes from Jemez Springs. The hotel and baths were managed by a man named Frenchy, and he did quite well.

About 1928, the hotel burned to the ground, and Frenchy was ousted and disappeared. The place lay abandoned for several years, except that my father would lease it in the summer months. We also built cabins—12 in all—for the health-seekers to live in. The family members took turns operating the bathhouses (one for men, one for women). There was an open- air pool for those who wanted to soak their feet and legs, and it was free. We charged 50 cents for a bath and sweat-box. An attendant had to be there, as the water had to be cooled in the tubs before each bath. We never charged any of our neighbors, or anyone who seemed poor, and there were many who came poor and broke.

The curative powers we witnessed were disbelieved then and are joked about even today. The easy things like head lice could be stamped out, eggs and all, in one dunking, as well as athlete's foot, never to return again. Boils and skin infections of any kind would disappear in a couple of days. We used to bring our horses who had wire cuts boiling with maggots.

15

We'd put the horse's foot in a bucket of warm water and it would heal in a few days.

There were many little springs, hot and cold, with varying amounts of sulphuric acid, which people drank for internal infections such as ulcers. We had a parade of people with venereal diseases, and they would be cured in a week. The alcoholics: a week to get their heads back on straight. The warm waters and quiet times were such a help to the arthritis and rheumatism sufferers. We saw at least one man come in on a stretcher carried by friends. He bathed freely and after three weeks, he walked out to Jemez Springs carrying his stretcher under his arm. Somehow, the sulphur does not harm live flesh, though it is strong to the taste and will eat holes in your clothes (except wool) and turn the coins in your pocket black.

When I returned from the Pacific as a foot soldier, the first thing I did was soak my bleeding feet at Sulphur Springs to get rid of the dreaded jungle rot we all got. There are soldiers today in the veterans' hospitals, unable to walk, with rotting feet. Some *did* go to the Springs to kill the disease, and never had it again.

In 1934, a man named Culler bought the Springs and built another hotel. It was small, but he had the advantage of REA Rural Electrification Administration, which gave him running water, electric lights and an improved road. In about 1975, the football coach at UNM and his assistant bought the by-now-defunct Sulphur Springs with tumble-down buildings. They started restoration, but in about 1980, the last hotel burned. There is a locked gate there now.

Many of us bathed in and drank the water. Most lived into their 90s.

This story appeared in the Jemez Thunder, *May 15, 1999.*

◀▶MINERALS OF THE JEMEZ MOUNTAINS ◀▶

Many years ago, perhaps in 1910, there was a mining town called Copper Canyon. It was in Señorita Canyon as it climbs out of Cuba on Highway 126 on the way to Rio de Las Vacas en route to La Cueva. There was a smelter there where they melted the copper for shipment. The coal they used came from La Ventana—Albuquerque's coal supply for nearly 100 years. Around the turn of the century, two young prospectors came ready to hunt gold, but worked at the copper mine. They found that the mine was now shutting down and decided to go into the Jemez country on their own and spent several years covering the Jemez Mountains. They found a lot of copper, especially on the ridges between Rio de La Vacas and La Ventana, but not rich enough to mine. It was later claimed by others, though there never were any worthwhile claims.

They found that the Spanish had copper mines on the west side of the Indian reservations and probably used Indian help to mine and bring it out. They found a good copper mine just north of the Guadalupe turnoff in the Jemez canyon. It was claimed by the Burnett copper mine, and it was going well when we came there in the 1920s, but shut down during World War II. They went on up the Jemez canyon looking for gold. They kept finding turquoise, but a poor grade. Although turquoise is made of hydrated copper and other phosphates, it was soft here and not good for jewelry.

They found a large deposit of lime to make cement. They followed the rivers and their branches, but no gold!! There were some ranches here that raised cattle. They found Sulphur Springs, and it did have commercial sulphur. There was also volcanic glass on the ridges above Spence Hot Springs that the Indians used to trade to other tribes, as well as a certain kind of clay to make pottery that came from our old ranch. Finally, they made their way across Jemez to Los Alamos and down in a deep canyon below Los Alamos and above Cochiti Pueblo.

They had planned to continue on to Cerrillos where gold could be sifted from the dry sand. The Cerrillos mines had been mined for turquoise for hundreds of years to supply the Aztecs and others with the best stones. The only other stones of this quality were found near Gallup.

The miners stopped in Bland Canyon and worked a fabulous claim. The canyon was steep and isolated and no roads, so the only gold had to be packed out to a buyer in Santa Fe. Men with money soon saw the gold and formed the Cochiti Mining Co. and bought these two out. The first partner took his cash and disappeared, the second hung around for a while and then he left. The mining company built some roads and put in three stamp mills and all the things a good mining company needs.

My grandfather moved his sawmill down from Glorieta and made all the timbers for the mine. He also made all the lumber for the houses and commissary. Quite a town sprang up, and the mine was the richest in New Mexico. One day the shaft met a blank wall. The engineers came and dug up and down to the right and left. The vein they were following just quit—perhaps a shift in the mountains—and it was gone.

The town died down and everyone left. It broke my grandfather, and although we lived there for many years—my brother was born there—we left also. The Hofheinses, Crandells, Kings and Fettersons and several others wound up in or near La Cueva.

In 1934, an Indian came into the Pueblo of Jemez and showed the storekeeper at the mercantile that he had a huge nugget that he had found on the Indian reservation just west of the pueblo. We went down at midnight and had a look. It was a long trip in the dark, and we were apprehensive. We found the mine, but the entrance was caved in. We dug it out and followed the tunnel a little way, and saw that the tunnel had been blasted out with black powder: It was a mine to recover copper. The Indian with the nugget disappeared.

This story appeared in the Jemez Thunder, *September 1, 1999.*

◄►VOTING IN THE OLD DAYS ◄►

In 1928, when we were voting for Herbert Hoover, we got the family together for a rough ride to Jemez Springs so we could vote, pick up the mail, and buy gasoline and groceries. We left early enough to do these things, and before we reached Jemez Springs, we were stopped near Via Coeli. The town marshal met us there carrying a .30-30 rifle and forbid us to go any further.

It seems that a culvert had been washed out and had narrowed the road to a one-way passage. The town marshal said the road was unsafe for us to cross over. My father, mother and we four children could walk the rest of the way to Jemez Springs so we could vote. My father was livid, as we met cars crossing the bridge, coming both ways. Now we knew we were Republicans, and have been ever since. For the last 70 years we have voted for the best man, regardless of party affiliation, but have always retained our Republican status.

My father turned our Model T around and went all the way back to the ranch and got his .30-30 and headed back down the road. After four hours on the road and a flat tire, we approached the bridge, and the marshal was gone. We sailed across the bridge and went to vote. The voting was taking place in a little store front, but as we got there the people at the polls said the polls were closed because no one else came

19

in to vote. Although it was early, the ballots had already been sent to Bernalillo, the county seat, and by now were on their way to Santa Fe.

We were cheated, and nothing could be done. In the next presidential election, my father took his gun with him, but there was no trouble, except the leaders kept out of sight of the polls, and gave a big drink of wine to some of the loafers and another drink when they voted.

We have always studied the candidates and ballots very carefully and gone to the polls early—a duty that every American should exercise.

This story appeared in the Jemez Thunder, *January 1, 2001.*

◄►VOTING IN THE OLD DAYS: PART 2 ◄►

When I read "Voting in the Old Days" by my brother, Joe Routledge, I decided to write the rest of the story. Our father was a staunch Republican, but he also kept an open mind and often voted a split ticket. Art Routledge continued to exercise his right to vote, even after the problems he encountered in 1928. He apparently voted more often than we knew.

Daddy knew practically everybody in Sandoval County and was respected by most. He was well-acquainted with the politicians, and they frequently flagged him down to discuss their policies. They knew that friends and neighbors often asked for his opinion. This was in a time when many did not have access to a newspaper or did not speak English. When friends and neighbors asked for his opinions, he tried to be objective. Daddy passed away in March of 1942.

In 1957, our family was living in Bernalillo. My husband, Alex Hill, had two brothers Sam and Swede, who were very active in the Republican Party. Sam served as a State Legislator for several years. That year, Swede was a Vigilante during the election. He told us my father was still a registered voter and had, in fact, voted in that very election!

This story, by Dorothy Routledge Hill, appeared in the Jemez Thunder, *February 1, 2001.*

◀▶ JEMEZ INDIAN IRRIGATION ◀▶

We have known that the Pueblo of Jemez has used water from the Rio Chicita and the Jemez River to irrigate their chiles and corn forever and ever. But no one has ever seen them dig their ditches or engineering the flow to the fields. Once a year, they clean the ditches, which is a community effort shared by all the men. We don't know how old some of these ditches are. We assume that the knowledge of engineering and the tools required were forgotten a long time past.

Their fields have not needed new ditches for a long time, but the Indians were put to a test some years ago. Steve Edsall owned a nice little ranch on the Peñas Negras (once owned by actor Hugh O'Brien), where he grew a hybrid barley that had been imported from Canada. Barley never grew at this altitude until he brought in the hybrid. Steve used a lot of Indian labor to harvest his crops, and he began to think about a little truck garden, if he could get water out of the Peñas Negras Creek to water the garden. He stopped at the pueblo and sent word that he wanted an irrigation ditch dug. The next week, he picked up a couple of old-timers and a young buck who said they could build him an irrigation ditch. He then put them in the bunkhouse and gave them a plow and shovels.

21

The first day they spent walking and viewing the land. The next day, they built a small dam upriver to take part of the creek water. Then they began to dig, part of it by plow. Steve knew enough to leave them alone and not watch.

Once he came down when the ditch was half finished and was curious that they were making a lot of headway. He saw that they had some sticks with a fork, like an old-fashioned sling-shot, and some straight sticks they were using, but they were not inclined to show their use. They smoked and talked as long as Steve was there, but never explained what the sticks were for.

In a week's work, they had finished the main ditch which was a little above the garden spot, and it was easy to see that any-one could water the rows below. All of us wondered how the ditches could be dug without modern instruments of any kind and flow freely down the ditch as it followed the contours of the land. Some of the ditch needed to be taken out a little if it was shallow, and some of the side walls needed building up. But the thing handled a reasonable flow the very first time it was used. Quite a feat, with a practiced eye and some sticks. The old Indians still have the engineering knowledge to irri-gate their fields.

This story appeared in the Jemez Thunder, *March 15, 2000.*

◄►THE FISH PLANT ◄►

In the early days of homesteaders in the upper Jemez Moun-tains, there were some streams and rivers that did not contain fish. While most of the streams were filled with cutthroat trout, some had never had any fish in them.

When E.M. Fenton (later called Grandfather Fenton) was dis-charged from the U.S. Army as an officer and a Presbyterian minister, he held some warrants that entitled him to public domain. He took up a huge piece of land that began just below what is now Fenton Lake and extended up the Cebolla. Mr. Fenton's brother homesteaded Barley Canyon, east of the Cebolla creek. Mr. Fenton's son, Mack, who everyone knew, later homesteaded up near the Seven Springs hatchery. So at one time, the Fentons owned or controlled the whole canyon from Fenton Lake to the Seven Spring hatchery.

Grandfather Fenton was a grand old man and held the love and respect of all the people around him. He prospered on his place, but it was too far upcountry to visit him or for him to export anything he raised, although the land was good. The only entrance to his ranch was up the Guadalupe through Cañon. At the place now called Gilman, there was a box canyon and very hard to get by on either side. There were horse trails coming in from the north side through the Valle Grande and Cuba. Another horse trail came through the Routledge ranch via Thompson Ridge and over Fenton Mountain. Also a road of sorts started at the Hofheins's place at La Cueva. The road was rough and was for buckboards as it went over Fenton Mountain via Deer Creek.

Mr. Fenton observed that none of the creeks or rivers in his area had fish in them, a real blow to a devoted Izaak Walton and gentleman fly fisherman. He was able to see that the falls in the box canyon on the Guadalupe prevented the fish from going up into the streams and rivers above. The large pool below the falls was boiling with cutthroat trout, and Mr. Fenton set out to correct this situation.

He brought his camp gear down to the falls and, using barbless hooks and fish worms, caught as many as he could. He had two five-gallon lard pails, and he put the live fish in these two pails with water. He packed these on a mule and then led him up the rocky trail around the falls. Here he dumped them in the river and went back for more. We can only speculate on the number of fish, and we think he spent two days on this project. It took a while, perhaps several years, before the fish plant was easy to see.

Fish went up the river and up the Rio de las Vacas, the Cebolla, the Calaveras, and the Peñas Negras, and any other little trickles that entered these water flows. Especially did they flourish in the several miles of the Cebolla, a natural hatchery with meadows and a wandering water with so many cutbanks. The black earth furnished plenty of worms, and summer brought grasshoppers and bugs galore. As a rule the fish were topping out at 12 inches, although once in a while someone would catch one at 16 inches. This area became the best fishing anywhere in New Mexico.

An example of the quantity was often told by Mack Fenton. When he was about 12 years old, his father had built a nice two-story rock house near Fenton Lake. Mr. Fenton had invited some important people up from Albuquerque to visit him and, after a hard trip to get there, Mr. Fenton thought a banquet of wild cutthroat trout would be a treat. He sent Mack out to catch a string of trout. Mack came back that evening with 50 good-sized trout. Mr. Fenton complimented his son on such a catch, but in a kindly way said "Son, I think we caught too many. I think we ought to limit ourselves to 25. We are the only ones fishing now, but there will be more as the country is settled. Let's tell everyone to take only 25 each day"

Mr. Fenton's words were prophetic. When fishing limits and licenses became law, we were all allowed 25 fish, and it stayed that way for years. Finally, it went to 15 and then to 10, where it remained for many years. I think we used to pay $2 for a license after age 12.

24

The fish hatchery at Seven Springs came before World War II, and before that was the Ranger Station. The Flukes family lived there, and they also handled the telephone exchange for Jemez Springs in their own home just down the road from the post office.

The fishing was good all through the mountains for 60 years. But we never had the pressure of good roads and a nearby city that grew from 50,000 to 500,000.

The story appeared in the Jemez Thunder, *January 15, 2000.*

◄►MY TRIP TO TOWN IN 1928◄►

Back in 1928, we leased the land next to ours—50 acres of it. I do not know the reason or much about it, but we spent the time and money to lease the place and planted it all in potatoes. It was a good idea on my dad's part, and he made a lot of money on the investment. Seemed like a lot of money for potatoes!

I do not know how he knew, but in Albuquerque they were selling for one dollar for 100 pounds, so a gunny sack of potatoes was worth one dollar! Although we had a lot of work plowing, planting and planning, it finally materialized in the fall, and we began to take those potatoes into town. We made enough money to buy a new Chevrolet flatbed truck. At that time, a new truck cost $400 to $600. As quickly as we could, we would take another load into town to sell. We had a bumper crop that year. Nevertheless, each potato had to be picked up and put into sacks, and they grew very close together, so it was no easy job.

My father had been taking potatoes into town all along, and he could make the round trip to Albuquerque all the same day. He had relatives there, so he would stay with them for the night. Most of the trips were a day in and day out, and he had a place to unload while there.

We kids never got to go to town very often, but my dad promised us we could make a trip with him if we worked hard. So, we got a chance to go, and it was really something special. My brother went first, and he got a new hand-tooled saddle for his trip. He was very impressed with this brand new saddle.

The next trip was my turn to go. Finally, the time came, and we loaded a big load of potatoes and started to town. When we got as far as Cañon, we found that the steep hill that goes down the canyon was strictly a low gear thing. As we started up the other side, the truck stalled and would not pull this load. There was only one thing to do, and that was to unload enough of the potatoes so he could proceed. The clutch was really slipping, and he needed to get to a mechanic to get it fixed.

We unloaded the potatoes at the side of the road. I was dressed in my Sunday clothes to make this trip, but my dad told me I had to stand by the potatoes and to see that no one, regardless of what, took any of them. He went on down to San Ysidro, where there was a mechanic that maybe could help him. I stood there for a long time waiting for him to come back.

In an hour or two, a man came by in a flatbed truck. He stopped and told me that my dad said for him to load all the potatoes up. I said to him that my father told me not to let anyone take these potatoes, no matter what. Well, I got on top of the stock with big tears streaming down my face, being only eight years old. I was scared to death of this big man, but I was there to fight! He finally felt sorry for me, and got in his truck and left. I didn't know it at the time, but he was sent back to pick up me and the potatoes and catch up with my dad in San Ysidro. In the meantime, I felt like I had saved the day! But on the other hand, I was scared to death.

Finally my dad had the clutch fixed and came back for me. He was a little upset, but we got on our way to Albuquerque. When we arrived, we went to the store and unloaded some of the potatoes. From there we went to Korber's Hardware and Implement Store, the biggest and best in Albuquerque. Across Tijeras Street was the wagon yard where we always parked our wagon and kept the livestock when we came to town. We parked our truck in there and went over on Copper Avenue to Mora's Saddle Shop. My dad had bought my brother's saddle there, and I was very proud that I had inherited the old saddle, which was really something special for me to have. It was in fine shape.

While we were there, we bought some leather goods and my dad bought me a pair of leather chaps. They were a little too long and dragged on the sidewalk when I went down the street. But they were brand new and the first pair of leather chaps that I ever owned. I was mighty proud of them!

Then we went back to Korber's to buy some 6- or 8-penny nails. I had never seen any new nails and never been in a place like this—row after row of pretty shining nails, and brick spikes 10 inches long. As we went down the line, the containers got smaller and smaller, and the last one had shingle nails. I was so intrigued by it all and had never taken anything in my life. I could not resist. When no one was looking, I reached in the bin and took a handful and put them in my chaps pocket and closed the flap. They were such a treasure!

From there we went to the courthouse. The city fire department was in the basement. Upstairs the mayor and all the city people had offices. My father knew a lot of the people. His

27

aunt was married to the fire chief, Art Westerfield, so we went to his office and paid a visit. He also knew the mayor, Clyde Tingley, and the police chief. The police force had a Model T touring car for their transportation, so, of course, my dad wanted to see it. He took me across the street to the police station, and all of a sudden, I thought about the nails in my chaps' pocket. I was scared to death and wanted to leave, but they thought I was cute, and my chaps looked good on me, so they were getting a kick out of me.

Then we went to my aunt and grandma's house and spent the night. The next morning we loaded up the truck with supplies for the ranch and went home. What a wonderful trip I had! However, I took the shingle nails out of my chaps pocket and hid them away. To this day, I do not know where they went.

Next it was Dorothy's turn to go to town, and she ended up with a brand new saddle and a lot of other things that all of us wished we could have had. That year, 1928 was a good year for us. The bumper crop of potatoes really paid off. Two new cars, new saddles, all our debts paid off, and we were secure financially. I never got another trip to town, but I will never forget the one I made.

This story appeared in the Jemez Thunder, *May 15, 2001.*

◄►LONG LOOK BACK AT LA CUEVA ◄►

La Cueva has been settled a long time. It is the birthplace of the Jemez River, where the Sulphur/Redondo and the San Antonio merge, and runs some 70 miles until it empties into the Rio Grande. Even though it picks up the East Fork, the Guadalupe, the Chicita, and the Rio Salado, the Jemez River is still without name change. La Cueva in the early days had three families, all living on the west side of the San Antonio River. Later the renowned lawyer from Albuquerque, a Mr.

Shields, built a cabin for his getaway further up the San Antonio and on the east side. All of them except Shields had to ford the river to get home.

On up the canyon toward Sulphur and Freelove, across the valley where the Thompson Ridge road takes off, there was an old homestead called the Kelly place, later to be called the White place or the fox farm, where George and Ben White built a two-story house with some sheds, and attempted to raise mink, and later silver fox. Neither enterprise panned out, so the family turned to logging.

Behind the White/Kelly place there had been a large enterprise with fields and log cabins that we called Mormon Flats. It was on the old Baca Location and dated back to the 1880s. There were traces of an old wagon road that went to El Cajete. When ownership of the Baca property was proven and fenced, the Mormons were forced to vacate.

Now I see the old Kelly place has many houses on it and is sometimes referred to as La Cueva. To me, it should be called Redondo or Kelly or Upper La Cueva. Even the little valley west of Sulphur Creek is being built on. It was once a sterile patch of ground covered by a foot of white sulphur clay and cut up by deep gullies. It seems there had been a 100-year flood originating above the Sulphur, and it brought all this bad refuse down the canyon. Not even weeds grew from our lower fence for some 40 acres below.

When the Civilian Conservation Corps (CCC) came in the 1930s, they made this a project. The young men brought good dirt by wheelbarrows and filled the ditches with rocks and tree branches. They planted trees and bushes, fenced the whole thing, and called it the reclamation project. No livestock was permitted to eat the newly-sown grass, posted as "restricted

29

area." In the more than 60 years since, the little valley has completely recovered.

As kids we explored the cave there. At one time, there was a little sawmill and a pond. Blocks of ice sawed from the pond would keep all year in the sawdust pile. Ice was a luxury in those days, and used only to churn the ice cream on the 4th of July. There was a place beyond Thompson Ridge where a cave was filled with ice each winter, and we could chip it out and take it away in a gunny sack to make ice cream in the summer. Otherwise, we had to depend on summer hailstorms, when we would gather the pellets in a wash tub. We sometimes made ice cream in the winter, when ice and snow were plentiful, but it wasn't as much fun as in the summer.

This story appeared in the Jemez Thunder, *April 1, 2000.*

RANCH LIFE

Art builds log house while Herb blocks log with rock.
1922

◄►COUNTRY KIDS◄►

My brother and I never had hardly any toys to play with, as town was three days away, and we just could not afford them anyway. Christmas time was the only time for the few presents we got. However, there were plenty of chances to play games of our own. We would play "rodeo" and ride the calves and get a few bruises. If we got caught, it would call for a good spanking by my protective dad.

We played a game that called for cow manure at 15 feet. We threw cow dung dried in the sun. Sometimes we were closer or further away as the flops were better dried and would reach farther. As we chased each other around the barn, the range got closer as the cow flops got fresher and harder to throw. The best score was to find one that had a big black beetle or two in it and throw it on your opponent. We had fun until the ammunition got too fresh, and we would have the green manure on our clothes. Mom would scold us when she washed them in a tub and hung them out to dry.

One of our favorite games was to gather a chicken apiece and throw them out of the third story window of the big hay barn. We had some pigeons that roosted in the barn, and in the daylight they sat in a row on the top of the barn. My brother and I would throw a couple of rocks at the pigeons, and they would immediately fly and circle the barnyard. This was an alarm that chicken hawks or an eagle were about to carry our hens away. The chickens ran for the henhouse and hid themselves from danger. My brother and I would shut the henhouse door and now we could catch any chicken we wanted. My brother selected a big Rhode Island Red, and I picked a nice, plump Plymouth Rock. We took them to the high window and threw them out. Chickens would only go 50 to 75 yards, as they are poor flyers. They always landed on their breast bone and turned a flip or two. My brother beat me at this game, so we went back to the henhouse and got two more! This time I selected a White Leghorn—she was a little skinny but had good wings. My brother selected the Rhode Island Red who was a winner, but the White Leghorn beat her easily, as we noted the distance from the barn window to the corral. We laughed as the fluttering chickens barely recovered their senses. We soon ran out of White Leghorns, as they were not as good layers as the Plymouth Rock or the Rhode Island Red, so we only had a few.

In the meantime, our sister Dorothy told my dad about sailing the chickens. We barely escaped a good spanking when my dad found out about this thing, even though he had removed his belt and threatened us both. He said, "Don't you know that throwing the chickens out the barn window would cause the chickens to break an egg inside of them and they would die?" We still thought the exercise was funny, and I bet my dad was mystified that we could do this. Boys will be boys!

This story appeared in the Jemez Thunder, *October 15, 2001.*

◄►BACKHOUSES ◄►

All the people who lived in Sandoval County had "back-houses," as no one had electricity or plumbing in their houses. Some people called them toilets, but our fathers all called them "shit houses."

Every ranch that had people living on it all had a backhouse in back of their house and never in front. These little buildings, no bigger than a phone booth, really took some ingenuity and planning to build. They always had a slanted roof covered with tarpaper, but they all must have ventilation up near the top, usually a shape cut like a quarter moon or even a star. The building had a wood floor and a raised seat for comfort. Most of them had two holes and sometimes three for the children. Also the holes were cut to fit and if well-built were all sanded down to be more comfortable. The better-made ones each had a lid, and it was held in place by hinges, or in our case, by leather straps.

The door always opened in to keep it from blowing away in a storm. On the outside was a button that spun around on a nail and if someone was inside the button would be neutral, and it could be fastened from the inside by a latch. We had to dig a hole three feet wide and four feet deep, and the building was set on this hole and recessed a little to be sure the base was covered with dirt to keep out bugs and varmints.

If it could be arranged, the clothes lines, and perhaps the wood pile, would be between the ranch house and the toilet and would save the poor old housewife a lot of trips to the clothes line and the wood shed. The backhouse had to be moved two or three times as years went by, so a new hole was dug each time and the dirt from the new hole was used to fill the old one.

There were some elaborate toilets in Block's Hotel in Jemez Springs and the one in Sulphur Springs. A boardwalk went to the men's and women's; however, most hotels used chamber pots and nobody went outside. Some of the people who could afford it would have real toilet seats and lids. There was always a sack of lime and a scoop to use to keep down the smell and the flies. Others had only one hole and no door and a dirt floor. One time I went into one of the outhouses that had a dirt floor and found that a rattlesnake was coiled up there. I went to my car and got my pistol and that was the end of the rattlesnake!

34

When the snow was real deep and it was cold, we spent very little time in the backhouse. Every fall, Montgomery Ward would send us a new catalog, and we would study the old one that lay on the seat. (The boys were only interested in the girls' underwear page.) By wintertime, we were into the business section, and ready for a new catalog.

This story appeared in the Jemez Thunder, *March 1, 2002.*

◄►WE RESET THE OUTHOUSE◄►

As we finished the noon meal, my father came riding in on a sweat-soaked horse. He dropped the reins and put his chaps over the saddle as he strode in the house for a late noon-time meal. In a little while, he came out the back door and yelled at the kids to take his horse out to the corral. My sister jumped at the chance and my brother and I snickered as she tried to get up on the horse. He was too tall, so she finally gave up and led the horse away.

My father had gone to the outhouse that was across the backyard for his "daily constitutional." Dorothy brought the horse around, and my brother and I saw that the clothesline would just clear the horse's head. Our clothesline was made of telephone wire and mighty strong. It ran from the wood shed to the back side of the outhouse. When this old rope horse felt the line pull on his saddle horn, he dug in. He pulled the outhouse over on its back and dragged it half-way across the yard. The door flopped open!

My brother and I saw my father emerge from the biggest hole face first, as it was a two-holer. He had his pants at his shoe tops and was yelling, "*Whoa! Whoa!*" We laughed and laughed and hid in the woodshed until we threw up! He would have killed us. My father got the horse stopped and bawled my sister out for leading him under the clothesline.

Of course, we had to reset the outhouse and restring the clothesline. It had to be done once a year, anyway. Every time we drive a country road and see an outhouse in back, it brings tears to my eyes and a good belly laugh. Though it's been more than 70 years, it can still make me laugh out loud.

This story appeared in the Jemez Thunder, *March 1, 2001.*

◄► MAMA'S PIANO ◄►

When our mother married, she was part of a family that was used to the finer things in life. She was part of the Cornells that founded Cornell University. Among her finer things was a big, black and beautiful upright piano of the best quality. She learned to play the piano early. When she was a teenager, she was playing for the services at the Congregational Church across the street from their home. She also taught piano to some of the children in the neighborhood.

When she married, she chose a wild, uneducated cowboy, and they wound up on a dirt wagon road. The marriage produced four children. The piano was left behind in storage, and she missed it every day.

Since there were no neighbors and no schools, we were home-schooled and home-churched. Mama had dreamed of teaching her children to play the piano, and it would have been a big help for the home schooling. She was very church-oriented and thought we should know the Sunday school songs and the church hymns. Alas, there seemed no practical way to get the piano to the ranch. Much argument and downright fussing at our father—who didn't think we needed the thing—caused him to give in and make the six-day round trip to town in our farm wagon to bring it home.

36

In Albuquerque, the piano was crated in a felt-lined piano box and then laid on its back on the bed of the wagon. After three days of bumpy road, it was uncrated without a scratch anywhere. Our mother's joy was a sight to see, but soon turned to tears when she pressed the keys. The piano went "boing, boing" and "clack, clack."

The 75 miles of rutted road on an iron-tired wagon had detuned it completely. Mama kept it polished and wiped her eyes when she walked by it. There was no way that a piano tuner would ever make the long trip by horseback to the ranch, and of course an auto could not reach us. In any event, we could never pay what the fee would be. We held school around the piano and sang our little church songs, but without music. But we did pray each Sunday for the piano to get well.

Our ranch was near the well-established horse trail that ran 200 miles across New Mexico from Fort Union to Fort Wingate at Gallup. And while we lived in an isolated area, we sometimes had interesting visitors whom we always fed and bedded for the night. Some were just traveling through, and some were very tight-lipped about their business on the road. However, we kids heard some wild stories from these drifters and relished a visit from anyone who happened to stop at our lonely ranch.

One fine summer day, a gent arrived riding a nice horse. He was a "dude," a city man dressed in a town suit. It was evening, and our father was still not home. We made him welcome and tended his horse while he made his way to the house to wash up and get ready for supper. While he waited, and my brother and I watched and snickered at his dress, he wandered over to the piano. He lifted the lid, tapped a few keys and cringed at the sound that came out. He hunted up my mother in the kitchen and said, "Your piano seems to be out of tune." My mother's eyes filled with tears as she explained how this came about. He said, "I happen to have my piano tools with me, and I think I can put it in tune for you." He walked down to the tack room where we had put his saddle and took a bundle from the saddlebags. He returned to the piano and rolled out a complete tool set, including tuning forks.

Now we began to pay attention. We were all eyes and ears as he began to work tightening the wires, and my mother was again near tears. She was so impressed with this handsome young stranger that was heaven-sent.

About this time, my father arrived after chasing wild horses since 4 a.m. with no lunch. He was hungry and upset that supper was not on the table. He listened while my mother told the good news and only wanted to know how much it would cost. The stranger said it would cost nothing and was a fair exchange for his bed and food and grain for his horse. After supper, the man continued his work while Mama did the dishes and we kids watched. Dad soon sent us all to bed and told the stranger he would not see him in the morning and hoped he could fix the piano and have a good trip. Dad was up and gone again at 4 a.m.

We had an early breakfast. Mama, dressed in a fresh dress, put on a deluxe meal. Then she and the man began to work on the piano, which was now coming into tune. We kids were intrigued by this sweet, sweet music. We finally went out to do our chores and realized there would be no school that day, so we went to play in the creek. When we came in at noon, there was no lunch for us, but mama said to have some bread and milk which we did with double helpings of sugar. The piano was now in perfect tune. Mama had dug out all her classical sheet music, and they were taking turns showing what they could do. Both were very good.

Late that evening, Papa came in after a full day in the saddle. When he saw the stranger's horse in the stall, the air began to turn blue with profanity. All us kids hid and tried to remember if he had his gun on. The piano was pounding out one of the fastest and latest tunes, and the two were playing a duet. Breakfast and lunch dishes were still on the table and nothing on the stove for supper. Dad burst into the house shouting, "Is that s.o.b. still here? Get out! Get out before I kill you!" My mother screamed back while the man rushed to pick up his tools and out to the corral to saddle his horse. It was getting dark so he fled down the wagon road leading to Albuquerque with my father shouting after him.

Things were really tense for about a week. My parents were not speaking, and we kids were careful to do our chores and stay out of the way. But Mama had a smile on her face when Papa was not around. Of course, the whole thing blew over as we all went back to work. Mama could not walk by the piano without cuddling a few keys.

A lot of good came of the piano, as it was the only one in our whole mountain area. We began to have country dances, much to my father's delight. We bought the latest sheet music when someone went to town and tried to learn the latest dances, such as Turkey Trot and The Black Bottom. Most of all it gave our mother a new and useful tool for her home-teaching. We all got piano lessons, but there was no music in any of us, and we never got beyond "Chopsticks." On Sunday, Mama brought us downstairs dressed in our Sunday best, and we had Sunday school and sang hymns. The first few weeks, we gave thanks for our answered prayers and thought of the nice man that came out of nowhere to restore our piano. I don't know if we ever knew his name, and we never knew where he came from or where he went or why he was so far out of his element. One thing for sure: we never forgot him!

This story appeared in the Jemez Thunder, *July 15, 2000.*

◄►LOST CHILD◄►

In 1925 in the month of March our little sister Bettie was just past her second birthday. We had some sunny days and a chance to work on some of the farm machinery. Axle grease and oil were applied, and we kids were intrigued by the mixture of graphite and tar. Bettie managed to get a handful of the shiny grease. She was the youngest and caused my father to cuss. He sent her up to the house out of harm's way.

Time wore on, and it became chore time. We milked the cows, fed the chickens and slopped the hogs, and then closed things up for the night. Soon we headed for the house with milk and eggs. My brother and I took water pails to bring water from the spring and wood for the stove.

My mother was much surprised that Bettie was not with us. We searched the house because she had been sent there two hours before. She was not there. We had seen her start for the house, but she never arrived! My father lighted a barn lantern and since he was an excellent tracker, he went back to where we had seen her leaving us. He found her tracks in the dusty wagon road that ran down the canyon. They went past the house following the road. A quarter-mile away, there was a creek crossing, and her tracks went right into the shallow water. The tracks did not come out the other side. She must have waded a little downstream.

The tracks appeared again further down the road, but one shoe and sock were missing. He followed the track a little ways, but it disappeared on hard ground. Mom and dad took lanterns and circled the area, but no luck. It was March and freezing at night, and the forest was full of spooky wild animals. We had to find her soon, or she would not survive.

My dad saddled a horse and flew down the road to La Cueva where a large road crew was camped on the San Antonio as they hacked out an automobile road through the mountains. These hardy men turned out with lanterns and searched the mountains all through the night.

One among them was an Indian from Jemez Pueblo who was said to be the best tracker anywhere. He took the lantern and, on hands and knees, decided that Bettie had left the road and started to climb the side of Thompson Ridge. The pine needles and rocky ground stopped his tracking until daylight. By 10 a.m. he was half-way up Thompson Ridge. He found Bettie asleep in a bed of pine needles alongside a log. He picked her up, and she began to cry as he carried her down to the road and to the ranch. My mother almost fainted away, and she too cried.

The problem was, how to call all those tired and hungry men scattered for miles around. One man rode my dad's horse to La Cueva and retrieved a box of dynamite and set it off away from the house. My brother and I never forgot the loudest blast we ever heard. I believe it shook the canyon walls for a full five minutes. Everyone came in to what they believed was a corpse.

Bettie was not harmed very much. She was frostbitten on her hands and feet, especially the bare foot. She was hungry and sleepy, and although she could talk, all she did was cry when someone tried to get her to say what had happened to her.

Those brave and hardy men were given the day off as they trudged back to eat and sleep the rest of the day away. What could we say to show our thanks, especially to the Indian who everyone pointed as the best for years to come?

My brother and I were sent up on the hill to gather snow in a washtub. They soaked Bettie's frostbite in snow, which is a tried-and-true way to save the flesh. Her frostbitten skin did turn black and peel off, but in two weeks she was back to normal. My mother was a good Christian. As we had no church or school, we were home-schooled and home-churched. We prayed for her return and gave thanks on our knees that she lived.

Bettie never recalled the lost night or seemed to think about it. She did continue life as a very shy and quiet person, so we think it did change her a little. I cannot express the agony of our family to have a child lost in a wild forest at night. Then the miracle of having her returned to us whole!

This story appeared in the Jemez Thunder, *February 15, 2001.*

◀▶ WILD MUSHROOMS ◀▶

The mountain people ate the things that came their way, especially if they were free. We harvested the wild berries such as raspberries, gooseberries, strawberries, and choke cherries, plus onions and mushrooms. There were greens called ground weed and lamb's quarters and parsnips, and a little game in season. Our grandparents and our parents knew the wild things to eat and when to pick them.

I remember when the wild onions came out in the summertime; our milk cows went crazy for them and would eat them all day for about a week. Our milk tasted like onions, and we threw it to the hogs. In late summer, we had a sudden crop of mushrooms, as they came out from under the pine needles.

Some of the big ones grew to a couple of pounds. We observed that the cows ate them until they were all gone, but it didn't affect the taste of the milk at all. Chipmunks and squirrels and birds all ate them, and these were the ones we picked.

We had an influx of town people that made the hard trip up here to pick the mushrooms. One of them was Senator Domenici and his family, most of Italian descent. They seemed to pick everything, toadstools and all, and put them out on a canvas to dry for winter use. There was a grandpa who spent the days gathering and occasionally threw out the poisonous toadstools, but all the others were good. We didn't have the knowledge, so we ate only what our parents and grandparents ate. All the mountain people ate this kind, and they were very good.

One late summer, Mack and Alice Fenton picked a bunch of the kind we knew were safe, didn't let the kids pick any, and sorted them a second time. During the night, Mack began to throw up, and found the rest of the family semi-conscious. He knew at once it was the mushrooms. There was not any help except for his dad, E. M. Fenton, who lived nearby. Mack thought if he could stay awake long enough, his dad might help. He found the keys on a nail and staggered out to his Dodge truck. There were a lot of keys, and he tried them all several times before he found the right one.

It was three miles on a crooked dirt road to his dad's place, but somehow he never got stuck, even though he kept running off the road. He finally pulled the battered truck into his dad's yard and laid on the horn. Mr. Fenton came out and realized that Mac's family might all be dead. He turned the truck around and flew to Mack's house. He found everyone alive, and roused them all and gave them a solution of salt water. They heaved and heaved, but two days later they were all fine.

It was a narrow escape, and all of us quit the mushrooms and never ate them again. Perhaps it was a hybrid of some kind. Later, as Mack and Alice ate a meal in town at the Court Café, they brought them a steak smothered in mushrooms. They could not eat it!

This story appeared in the Jemez Thunder, *February 1, 2000.*

◀▶ DEL MONTE PEAS ◀▶

In the 1930s, a new industry came to the Jemez. The officials of Del Monte came to our country and said that sweet peas of Del Monte fame would grow here. We agreed, as we already grew peas in our gardens and they were fine quality because of the short growing season.

The people of Del Monte arranged to lease or use all the hay fields of La Cueva and above, including El Cajete, to grow these sweet peas. They would furnish the planting and the seed, and the owner did nothing except to keep the livestock out. Nearly all the farmers and ranchers went for the deal except the Routledges, as we had considerable livestock, and we needed the tall oat hay to feed for the winter. The pea vines, after the harvest, were reasonable feed, but not good enough for our dairy cows and some of the others.

That spring all the fields were planted, and a disease-free crop was produced in king-sized Del Monte peas. At harvest time, the Del Monte people brought in pickers from everywhere. People from Oklahoma, Texas and other states came. All the local people had jobs.

Most workers went away for other crops, but some stayed for the next year's crop, meanwhile working in the log woods. I think we had two crops of peas, but the third crop was either frozen or ruined by hail. Many of the pickers were stranded here and turned to the log woods for a living. Some of the second and third generations of these people settled here and became loggers. One thing we gained from Del Monte: the grouse came by the hundreds and some still remain. There were so many that you could take a .22 and get all the grouse you wanted any time.

Del Monte did not try to use the Jemez again, as it was too high, though we had a fast growing season. In the meantime, Del Monte moved over to Blue Water beyond Grants and planted carrots that grew a foot long and as big as your wrist. They had a lot of land there, and they built one-room shacks, mostly for the Indian help. The crops grew for many years, and the help was there at harvest time.

We were not sorry we did not go for the peas, and saved much trouble to change our fields. Some said the peas did not do the ground any good. However, most people profited from the extra folks, and we could use the extra workers in the woods from time to time. Such it was with Del Monte. The ranchers, loggers and Indians took it in stride.

This story appeared in the Jemez Thunder, *October 1, 1999.*

◀▶ MEAT AND POTATOES DIET ◀▶

As ranchers with not much cash, we did not live off the land, but we took everything we could to eat. Since we had no refrigeration of any kind, all the small animals we caught to eat had to be consumed in one or two days. Some small sheep and goats were especially tasty if roasted. There were lots of rabbits and squirrels that were hunted by a boy with a single shot .22 rifle.

When we harvested our oat hay, the wild turkeys would come in large flocks, so we would have a lot of turkey to eat while harvesting. We hardly ever killed a deer unless it was in the fall and we happened to have a gun as we rode horseback. We preferred the beef cattle and "fatted" calf. When winter came, we would kill a large pig (porker), butcher it, and hang it up to freeze. With a good steer, and perhaps a deer, this was our meat for all winter.

We raised fields of potatoes and turnips. Potatoes were on the table at least once a day! My father cooked oatmeal every day for breakfast because it was so cheap, and we never seemed to tire of it. As we owned a cream separator, we had good whole milk and pitchers of real cream. Cottage cheese was easy to make. We would put the sour milk in dish cloths that were made from the sacks that our flour came in and hang them on the clothes line to drain. What curd was left inside was our cottage cheese. We also had real homemade butter, as we had plenty of cream to do the churning!

Our garden produced large heads of cabbage and lettuce that grew so well in the short summer season. We also grew carrots, the best peas (that had to be shelled), and rhubarb for our pies and other desserts. At certain times, the edible kind of mushrooms grew around in the forest. We picked them and ate our fill as long as they lasted—fried mushrooms, mushrooms in salad, and mushroom gravy. Very delicious.

Along with wild parsnips, lamb's quarters, and various other greens that we could eat, we had plenty of variety to supplement our diets. We lived too high in the mountains to grow tomatoes, corn, or strawberries, although in the summer time we could find wild gooseberries, raspberries, choke cherries and crab apples, and we sure ate our fill of those. It was a lot of work to find them to pick, but very worthwhile. When we would get a chance to go to Jemez Springs, we would buy some fresh fruit: plums, cherries, apricots and very good apples. They sure tasted good after all the meat and potatoes we ate at nearly every meal!

When we did butcher a steer for the meat, my mother used every part of the animal in some way. She made headcheese, fixed the tongue and sweet breads, brains and scrambled eggs—very good. She also made blood pudding, but that did not go over very well with the family.

We carried water from the spring up to the house in buckets for drinking and household purposes. There was no doctor for miles around. The closest one was in Albuquerque, two days away. Iodine, coal oil, and Vicks VapoRub kept us in good health.

My mother lived to be 94 years old. She had five children and did well all her life. Three of us are left: Dorothy in Roswell, NM; Bettie in Pomona, CA; and myself, Joseph, in Lakewood, CA. We are all in pretty good health in spite of all the bad drinking water and the meat and potatoes!

This story appeared in the Jemez Thunder, *August 15, 2001.*

◄► WHEN LIGHTNING WALKED ABOUT ◄►

When we were six years old, we were schooled about lightning. If you lived or worked at 9,000 or 10,000 feet, you knew the summer rain storms would bring a lot of thunder and lightning. Our parents and the old-timers gave the rules not to be hit. First, you must never be on the skyline, and you must be quick to find a place in the valley and under a small tree. Lightning hit the tallest trees, and especially those on the mountain tops or any rises or ridges nearby. If there was a house or shelter, get inside. Stay away from livestock and abandon any machinery that had iron or metal in it, and stay away from fences. When cars came, they were safe because of the insulated rubber tires.

But nothing is safe or faultless. Once I rode a horse across a meadow in the pouring rain. As we ran for shelter, a bolt hit nearby, and my horse went down. Although we were not hit, he trembled for a few minutes and then stood up unhurt. My sister Bettie ran out in the yard to retrieve her dolly and was thrown to the ground unconscious, but by the time we carried her to the house, she revived and was okay.

I have seen tall pines that were hit and splintered into pieces that weighed no more than 10 pounds. Usually a tree follows the bolt to the ground in a spiral, or it may split the tree in half. Many snags are made this way, but once a tree is dead, it seems free of another bolt. Lightning does hit twice in the same place, and we saw it happen at San Antonio Hot Springs where we used to bathe. A storm came up, and we ran for an old stone house there. We watched while it hit a pile of rocks above us two different times in less than 10 minutes.

The fire towers are legend, and I have been up in the one at Sierra Pelow and the one at Red Top where Mack Fenton spent much of his time. They are spooky, but they have an arrester that will carry a bolt to the ground. Some say that there is ground lightning, where a ball of light rolls along on the treeless desert until another lightning bolt picks it up.

I knew of four people hit by lightning. Two were sheepherders, and two were ranchers near the edge of the Baca Ranch. One was named Robert Lee and is buried there. This is the old Lee Ranch that is now leased to Jim Trehern. Another was a man named Ramsey who had his hand on a piece of equipment, but survived the bolt. The two sheepherders were killed near the center of the Baca Ranch. Someone came along and found their sheep scattered and the two dead herders in a camp under a small pine tree that had been used as a campsite for 50 years. You can never be sure.

They took my father's wagon and team to retrieve the bodies, which were wrapped in canvas and parked in our corral, awaiting their employer to come and take them to Bernalillo. Mr. Diego came in a Lincoln car and took them away. My brother and I were warned to stay away from the wagon, but we peeked anyway. I saw only burned clothes. I do not know what my brother saw, but we spooked and stayed away from the wagon.

In 1928, we bought a radio. Near our house was a tall pine tree and we used it for an antenna to the house. We had a lightning arrester to protect the house. A bolt of lightning hit the line and killed the tree. It did no harm to the house, but it trashed the radio. We had the barn dance on it only a few times. We never tried for a radio again. Also, the lightning came down the stovepipe, and we know not where it went then. We stayed away from the kitchen a long while during the summer rains. Those of you who have been out there, know you can smell a bolt if it hits nearby. It has an acrid, but not unpleasant smell. We do not hanker to live where there is lots of lightning.

This story appeared in the Jemez Thunder, *December 1, 1999.*

◄►A LOT OF BAD LUCK◄►

In 1917 and 1918, my father started a homestead in a little canyon (Media Dia) near Bland, just below Los Alamos. He had a team, a good double-bitted axe, and a saw. He cut down trees and dragged them to a level spot and built a log cabin on it all by himself.

It took all summer, and he installed my mother and my older brother, along with some chickens and a milk cow. From the milk, we could make butter, which could be traded at the mining company store in Bland for flour, sugar and lard. He had planted an open patch of ground in potatoes, and these would be harvested and also traded in Bland.

He built a corral, shelter, and fenced lot for the milk cow. The skunks ate his chickens, so they were kept under the porch of the cabin, but more bad luck was ahead. One morning, the cow was not to be found, and he thought she had wandered off. As my father looked around, he saw blood and drag marks on the ground and found huge footprints of a great bear. The bear had killed the cow and dragged her across the Media Dia Creek and uphill into some trees. The carcass was partially eaten—but no sign of a grizzly bear. No other animal had the power to drag a milk cow across a creek and up a hill. The tracks were there to see.

My father found himself on foot and unarmed near a grizzly bear's meal. He went back to the cabin, saddled a horse, picked up a rifle, and went back to the half-eaten cow. He found the bear's tracks leading away to the north. He followed them for a while, but they disappeared into the pine needles. He watched for the bear to return, but it never did. Everyone was sure that it had left New Mexico and was the last of the grizzlies in the Jemez Mountains.

My father ran into a lot of bad luck at this time. A horse kicked him and broke his leg. An amateur doctor set the leg, but it developed gangrene, and he had to be taken to Peña Blanca and put on a train for Albuquerque. His leg healed, but had to be broken again and reset, leaving him with a bad limp for the rest of his life.

In the meantime, he had been conscripted to serve in World War I. When he began to get well, he was sent to drive supply wagons into Mexico as they chased Pancho Villa. He and his army had invaded the little town of Columbus across the border into New Mexico. They killed some civilians and cleaned out the general mercantile store and headed back to Mexico. The U.S. Army never caught up with him, and he was assassinated in 1923.

My father's little homestead was abandoned, and he never went back. His relatives were told to take all his meager belongings until he was released from the army. When he did return, he was poorer than ever, but he started all over again in Freelove Canyon in 1920.

This story appeared under the title "The Last Grizzly Bear" in the Jemez Thunder, *March 15, 2001.*

◄►WHEN SOMEONE PASSES AWAY◄►

We lived a lot of years without a doctor in the mountains. Sometimes when people would pass away, there was no help at all for them. The mountain people lived a rough life, what with untamed livestock, horses, farm machinery, and logging, not to mention the narrow roads and other hazards that came with it. We learned that when someone passed away, you had to find a coroner to come and find out what happened—a long process.

One time Tim Hofheins came upon a man who was pinned underneath his Model A roadster, which had gone off a curve between La Cueva and Sulphur Canyon. Now he had to stop and get a ride into Jemez Springs and find a justice of the peace, as there were no police in Jemez Springs at the time. They went back to the scene of the accident and determined the cause of death. After the papers were filed and the reason determined, they could remove the body.

There were about seven deaths in the many years we lived there. One was this man, a more-or-less stranger to us. Another time, two sheepherders were struck by lightning, and it took two days to bring them into our ranch. A coroner from Bernalillo came and removed the bodies. Poor little Letha Hofheins died of appendicitis, but she was in Jemez Springs, and the priest gave her last rites. Then there was the truck driver whose runaway truck loaded with logs ran off the road below Spence Hot Springs. The trailer ran over the driver as he jumped to save his life. Sometimes, loggers would have a tree fall on them. Most were temporary workers. One poor guy fell out of the bed of a pickup truck near the Hummingbird Lodge.

The one that everyone felt the most was Ranger Lewis, a man we all loved, and he left several small children. His loaded pickup was pulling a trailer with a horse in it, and he went off the road when he was northbound, halfway to La Cueva above Spence Springs. It was quite a while before he was found, pinned in the wreckage. The poor old horse had put his neck through the trailer window and choked himself to death. My father died in the winter of 1942. The snow was so deep that we had to shovel it out so we could get the pickup out to Highway 4 and go to Jemez Springs for a coroner. He was buried in Albuquerque.

Life goes on. We were lucky and made it through the rough times unharmed.

This story appeared in the Jemez Thunder, *December 1, 2001.*

ANIMAL
ADVENTURES

Daisy, pet deer at Freelove Canyon ranch.

◄►A HUNTER WRESTLES A DEER◄►

A bunch of us were hunting above the fish hatchery on the Cebolla. We didn't have any luck all morning, so we met at the truck for lunch. We decided that since the weather was warm, the deer were high on the mountain and lying down in the shade. So after lunch we all headed for the high country. We split up, and Dave took an area that was away from the rest. He hunted the ridges and didn't find anything, and later in the day, he decided to carefully work his way down the mountain. When he was nearly down, he was surprised to see a 10-point buck get up from a sheltered bed and bounce away.

Now Dave was a good shot, and he fired. He saw the deer go down. He walked over to the buck ready to shoot again, but the deer lay still. So it was a fatal shot, although he saw no blood where the buck had been hit. He leaned his rifle against a tree and unsheathed his knife to bleed the animal by turning its head downhill. The bleeding is done by cutting both arteries in the neck. Just as he cut the first artery, the deer jumped to its feet and charged Dave with its head and horns down. Dave dropped his knife and grabbed the horns in both hands to keep from being gored. The 200-pound buck weighed as much as Dave did and pushed Dave rapidly down the hill. Dave held on. Once he thought he would be backed into a tree and impaled, but Dave gave way to the side. The front hooves of the deer were now starting to tear off Dave's shirt and pants, and it was all Dave could do, with outstretched arms, to keep him from going any deeper. Of course, Dave hoped the wound would bleed the animal to death, but it was only one jugular.

They were a bloody mess. Dave saw that the bullet he had fired was just behind the horns and had made the buck unconscious for a few minutes. The pair were now coming to a flat spot on the ground, and Dave, after a quarter mile of being on the down side, was now tired. He had the advantage of level ground and began to call for help, but none of the hunters heard him.

After a half-hour of mixing it up, the buck lay down, but Dave held on until he was sure it was dead this time. Dave went back for his rifle and knife and hoped the deer would still be there when he got back. It was, so he fired three shots, and the nearest hunters came to his aid. We were all astounded that his clothes were in ribbons, and he was a bloody mess. His ribs had only small cuts that nevertheless took a while to heal. All of us learned to be sure the deer was dead before we used the knife.

This story appeared in the Jemez Thunder, *October 14, 2000.*

◄►A STICKY PORCUPINE ◄►

In the old days, our grandparents and other old-timers used to say, "Never kill a porcupine." He is the only edible small animal that can be killed by a sharp blow on the head with a small stick. The story is true because if a man is lost in a trackless forest and does not have a weapon of any kind, if he comes upon a porcupine he can get a small stick and hit it on the head and have some food. Rabbits and squirrels are impossible to kill this way.

A porcupine is not afraid of man or beast, but just moves away. If molested, he puffs up his quills and draws his little pointed head under himself. His quills are his defense. His flat tail is covered with quills, and surprisingly, he darts around about as fast as a rattlesnake and hits everything that comes near him. This quick penetration has people believing he throws his quills, but this is really not true.

Porcupines live in the trees of a pine forest and will climb 10 or 15 feet up to eat the bark of the smaller pines. They are easy to find, as there are bright orange pellets in their area. They look just like Cheetos but are actually chewed up bark that has passed through the animal.

The Indians used porcupine quills to decorate their regalia and when men came with their cattle, the porcupine was left alone, and they were plentiful. The people who had cows found them to be very curious. They would stop and sniff the porcupine and get their snouts full of quills that had hooks on the end. The quills would bury themselves deeper and deeper until they choked the cow or they reached the heart or some vital part. If the cow was found right away, the quills could be pulled out with a pair of pliers. Otherwise, the cow could not eat well and may die in a few months. Ranchers' dogs always get a mouthful of quills, and the rancher pulls them out at once, but you can bet this dog never gets hit again. He just barks at them.

With the exception of the mountain lion, nearly all animals stay away from the porcupine. The lion knows what he must do and is able to slip a paw underneath the quills and rip the underside of the porcupine and turn him upside down. The underside is as smooth as buckskin, and the lion eats his carcass and then his quills. However, one time I ate over at Emmitt Smith's over on the Peñas Negras, and he and his lion dogs had killed a big male that had quills in his mouth and head.

Sometimes a motorist would run over a porcupine in the road, but the tires in the '20s and '30s soon developed slow leaks and a lot of flats until the tires were thrown away. We have eaten porcupine. Though the taste was not bad, it smelled like turpentine to most of us. One time I found three little porcupines that had no quills. They were soft and fuzzy and about the size of a small cottontail rabbit. I let them go free.

This story appeared in the Jemez Thunder, *February 15, 2002.*

◄►HORSES CAN SEE IN THE DARK◄►

In 1923 or 1924, we had our first automobile ride. Although it was a while before we had another ride, we have been crazy about them ever since. My father was the foreman at Los Alamos which, at the time, was a cattle ranch and later a boys' school. He arranged a ride for us to Albuquerque because we were little kids and my sister was a babe in arms. We spent the night in Albuquerque after a long and exhausting day traveling the dirt roads from Española to Santa Fe. We were amazed at the big powerful Willys Knight sedan that was owned by Mr. Shufflebarger, whose company had paved most of the streets in Albuquerque and could afford this machine! The next day we moved to Jemez Springs to stay with the Millers—a rough all-day trip in a car.

My father was trying to move his cattle and horses to our ranch in Freelove Canyon. It was spring, but a snowstorm still came in April. My father had sent a 16- or 18-year-old to drive our team to Jemez Springs. We stayed all night and loaded the farm wagon with all our gear for the ranch. Our team were good horses—one was snow white named Dolly and the other was black with a star on his forehead, named Star. We were late leaving Jemez Springs, and it was spitting snow. By the time we got to Battleship Rock, the snow was six inches deep. The farther we went, the deeper it got as we followed the San Antonio River on a bad road about halfway between Spence Hot Springs and La Cueva.

We became stuck on a steep hill that was called Stump Hill. The horses were tired and could not and would not pull the wagon any farther! It was late at night and none of us could see two feet in front of us in the swirling snow. It seems that we were stuck here for the night, and we would freeze.

My mother thought Dolly could find a way out. So they unhitched the team and took their bridles off and fastened the lines and the tugs up so they would not drag in the snow. Mother mounted Dolly, trying to keep my baby sister warm under her coat. My brother and I were cozy under a buffalo robe, but they took us out—he was six and I was three—and put us on Star. My brother was on the front, and I held on behind. The young man walked along side Dolly and held on to the tug strap so as not to lose his way. Dolly started up the road and never left the center all the way. It was so dark, none of us could see beyond the ears of our horses. We did not know where we were for about three hours, but old Dolly stopped at our barn door! We could not believe that she had pulled us nine miles through a blinding snowstorm.

The rest is easy: we unharnessed the team and put them in the warm barn. The house was empty, and the fire had been out for two days. We got warm and ate some warm soup and went to bed. Horses can see at night, and we escaped freezing in the deep dark river of San Antonio.

This story appeared in the Jemez Thunder, *November 15, 2000.*

58

◄►SKUNKS◄►

The Jemez Valley has a few skunks that only come out at night, so a few might be seen in the lights of the cars. Nowadays, most of the dogs are kept in the house and very seldom do they find one to bark or bite at. If you smell one, you may think it is passing through or just putting up stink. Unless the skunk is molested, it has no odor at all, and the stink it left behind is for its own defense.

My grandfather and my father and the other old-timers said that skunks carried hydrophobia, and they could and would give it to other animals. Also, they reached a pinnacle every seven years, and they were everywhere! At this peak of their existence, they became diseased, much like distemper in dogs, and all the skunks in the area died. It took seven years for them to make a comeback.

Our big old ranch dogs slept on the front porch and kept away all the coyotes, bears, wolves, raccoons, and whatever varmint came around. Nothing could defeat the ranch dog! In the winter, they slept in a doghouse, but they were always on the alert and any kind of disturbance would bring out a shotgun or rifle.

In 1936, the skunks came to us, and we found them under the building where they had nests and raised their young. As soon as it got dark, the skunks would come out and hunt until daylight, then return to their nests. Our dogs learned in one lesson to leave skunks alone. They would kill one the first time around and come out the worse for the wear, and you could smell him for a week!

One of our neighbors had a big, vicious Airedale that always smelled like a skunk. One time he killed a porcupine and was full of quills. Ben White knew they had to be removed, so he and his son held the 100-pound dog down and pulled them out one by one with a pair of pliers, despite his terrible stench. But some of the quills punctured his heart, and lungs, and he died. We had a lot of skunks and everyone, including the dogs and cats, left them alone. I can remember seeing a mama skunk one night walking along with five little ones right behind her all in a row.

Finally, one of our Holstein milk cows stepped on a skunk in the milk barn, and the fresh milk had to be fed to the pigs that day. All the buckets and utensils had to be washed and rinsed several times. My dad was very upset and designated me to trap all the skunks I could in the crude traps I had made to catch squirrels. They were called "figure four" traps. I baited them and put them in a bay at the far end of the milk house. It had a trap door at the entrance, and if it slammed, it kept everything in there. Skunks were easy to trap, as they would eat anything. When one was in the trap, I would take it down to the river, then go back the next day and take it out of the trap and bury it up on the hillside. There was no odor at all.

We discovered that when the skunk was in the trap, he was caught by the tail and could not "perform." One of our neighbors, Perris Linam, heard about this and tried it. Sure enough, as long as it was in the trap, there was no action. But as soon as he released it and its feet hit the ground, Perris was sprayed top to bottom! I accidentally let one spray me, and he got my jeans and shoes real good. I had to bury my jeans, but the brogans smelled in spite of the cow manure and etc. until they wore out.

That winter they did well, as they had a good fur coat. But as spring came, they all died off, and we never saw them again in La Cueva or Sulphur Canyon. Here's a little cat-like creature that has no fear of man or beast and is left alone at all times!

This story appeared in the Jemez Thunder, *September 15, 2001.*

◀▶CHICKEN THIEF◀▶

I woke in the middle of the night to hear chickens squawking, and—though the chicken house was some distance away, near the corrals—it was a disturbing noise to hear during the night. I had shut the chicken house door at dusk, so the only thing we could assume was that someone was sacking up the chickens and stealing them. So I pulled on my shoes and went downstairs and woke my father. He said we would teach that thief a lesson, and grabbed his double-barreled 12-gauge loaded with buckshot. I lighted the Bullseye barn lantern, and we headed for the chicken house.

On the way, I thought about our appearance as we marched for the corrals, my father dressed in night clothes as every old timer did at the turn of the century. He had on a nightgown (as did my mother) and a nightcap. (Remember "The Night Before Christmas?") So I just got tickled as I saw my father in unlaced brogans and a nightgown and cap, waving a shotgun. I was in my long-handles and boots.

As we approached the chicken house, we expected the door to be open and someone sacking up the chickens, as they were still squawking. But the door was closed, and a wooden peg held the hasp shut. While we considered this, I shined the lantern around the chicken house to see if someone had broken in. I shined the light on a knot hole and we saw a skunk stick his head part way out. Without a second thought, my dad fired both barrels at the skunk and blew a board off the side of the chicken house and scattered bits of skunk all over inside. The chickens flew around and began to sneeze and squawk and fight their way out of there. I opened the door and they came out, even though it was dark.

As we went back to the house, I was again tickled by our comic look, the rest of the family now awake because of the

61

blast. Now the dogs came out to see what we were doing. They had learned long ago to leave skunks alone, even if they were in the chicken house. The next day found me fitting a board to the side of the chicken house and shoveling out the chicken manure and bits of skunk. It made me throw up a little. We burned sulphur in the chicken house until the chickens would go in to roost.

I again laughed out loud at a grown man going to the corrals in a nightgown and cap in unlaced brogans, waving a double-barreled shotgun, and a youth in his long-handles and boots carrying a barn lantern. I was glad no one saw us as we hunted the chicken thief.

This story appeared in the Jemez Thunder, *May 15, 2000.*

◄►JEMEZ SPRINGS TURKEYS◄►

The Jemez Mountains were known for their flocks of wild turkeys. They were everywhere, but mostly in the higher mountains above Battleship Rock and to the north and west of La Cueva. There were many flocks of 10 to 30 birds. The most we ever saw was on Thompson Ridge, a flock we estimated to be 60 hens and gobblers.

The ranchers and homesteaders ate one once in a while. The grain fields the people planted drew the turkeys in great numbers, especially in the fall when the grain ripened and the horse-drawn mowing machines cut the oats and barley. A grain-fed turkey is really good eating, and the fact that we carried a shotgun to the field once in a while didn't deter them. There were more and more every year. All the ranchers felt that we could eat the birds we were feeding.

No one raised or kept turkeys because of the natural supply. We also learned early on that wild gobblers would sooner or later invade your farmyard and pirate your domestic turkeys anyway. The farm turkeys were always eager to go, and in a few minutes, every single one would join the gobblers' flock and be off to the high country. We would see them at times, but we had to shoot them if we wanted them back. Domestic turkeys do not roost in tall trees, but as they went wild, they'd try for smaller trees. When their chicks hatched, this generation could fly with the best of them.

There was a man who had a nice little place along with an orchard, on the Jemez River just north of what is now Hummingbird Music Camp. He was called a Gentleman Farmer, as he hired all his work to be done and never followed the walking plow. He was an expert at grafting fruit trees of all kinds and had the best orchard in the canyon. No fruit of any kind grew further north than here because of the altitude and the cold. This Gentleman Farmer wore tailored clothing and was friendly but aloof. It was obvious he had money and the best of education. My father seemed to know him well. His name was Howard Roland.

One summer he acquired a flock of white turkeys. We didn't know that turkeys came in white, and they were a great curiosity to us all. They were a little bigger than our wild turkeys and seemed to do well at Roland's place. That fall we had an early and wet snow in the high country and a lot of the wild birds migrated down out of the mountains to escape the snow and to harvest a bumper piñon crop. Now *there* is something good to eat: A roasted turkey that was fattened on piñons. I think you have already guessed that a wild gobbler and his flock descended on Mr. Roland and scooped up his white birds and headed for the rim. Thus began sightings of white turkeys that startled the locals to no end.

For the next 20 years, we saw white turkeys. The Fentons, Hofheins and Fettersons ate a white turkey once in a while, but we couldn't tell any difference in the taste. The white ones were the best targets. Even after the white ones were gone, there were mixed feather patterns everywhere. Mack Fenton killed a gobbler that weighed 24 pounds and was so big and fat he couldn't fly. The addition of the white bunch did not seem to add or subtract to the number of wild turkeys. We called them the Howard Rolands or Jemez Springs turkeys. During those years, our Forest Ranger, Harvey Barlow, never arrested anyone for killing a turkey out of season and loved to eat with us when we had turkey for dinner. A later Forest Ranger, Mr. Lewis, liked turkey up until the day he died.

We were not responsible for the turkey decline. As the Forest Service began to close our fields for lack of permits and as the country was logged, the population dropped. Also, new trapping laws caused the numbers of bobcats and coyotes to surge, and they got the rest. I haven't seen a wild turkey since 1980 when Jim Trehern and I killed a couple on the Rio de las Vacas—legally.

This story appeared in the Jemez Thunder, *February 15, 1999.*

◄►MAD DOG SCARE OF 1928◄►

In 1928, we had a "mad dog" scare. There were a couple of sheepherders in the Regina area who found something disturbing their sheep in the middle of the night, so the youngest (and least afraid) pulled on his pants and went to see about things. Before he got to the sheep, he was jumped upon by a wolf, and the wolf was going for the throat. The young man threw up his arms, pulled a knife from his belt and began to stab the wolf. They rolled on the ground, and he stabbed it many times. He finally killed it, but he was bitten many times about the head and left arm. He lay abed to see if he would get well, but finally rode a horse to Cuba to see a doctor. The doctor was away delivering a baby to a rancher's wife. So the young man took a room at Young's Hotel and went to bed. The people downstairs in the lobby were speculating on whether he had hydrophobia (or Mad Dog disease) that animals sometimes get.

Early in the evening, the man came downstairs. He was confused and angry and ready to combat anyone. The men in the lobby held a conference and felt they must do something before someone got hurt. They banded together and chased him back upstairs. They tried to bind his hands and legs with rope. There were some seven or eight men, but he was much too strong for them. They finally took a mattress off the bed and put him on the floor, covering him up, all of them holding the mattress down. After a while, he ceased to struggle and the men found he was quite dead. Some thought he had smothered. When the doctor returned, they held an inquest and found he had died from hydrophobia. About this time, we heard about the Cuba thing and we were aware that there was no cure for hydrophobia, but we thought it was a disease from the "flatlands," and we had never had it up here.

About this time, a big black dog came to our ranch and, of course, our dog Punch jumped him and sent him away. We thought we knew all the ranch dogs that other people had, but this one was new. We thought he came down the trail from Thompson Ridge, or from Fentons or the Valle Grande. When my father came home, he saw a crazed animal and immediately pulled his gun and put him away in three shots. We buried him, and put a chain on good old Punch, and locked him in a shed. I think he was in the shed for three days, and we were cautioned not to go near him. We were without the protection he gave our ranch.

One night at about bedtime, we heard Punch running around the house in a frenzy, across the full length porch. He had broken his chain and had escaped the shed. My father was not at home, but there was a brave young man staying with us named George. He lighted a lantern and crawled out on the roof. He took a .30-30, called the dog's name as he ran by, and the dog stopped for a moment—long enough for George to shoot once, and again to be sure.

The next morning, we rolled the dog onto a piece of canvas, being careful not to touch him. We dragged him a little way and dug a deep hole and buried him along with his collar and chain. We scrubbed the porch with lye soap. A sad ending to a faithful dog. We were all warned to stay away from animals that could bite. My brother and I and the rest of the family were warned not to get down on the ground away from the ranch. We got a new dog, but it was the scariest summer we ever spent.

This story appeared in the Jemez Thunder, *August 1, 1999.*

◄►A DEER NAMED DAISY ◄►

In the days when we ran cattle on Thompson Ridge and had a 99-year cattle permit on the forest, the Baca Location had a fence, but it was lying on the ground for long stretches in many places, so the livestock just grazed wherever there was good feed and water. It took a lot of horseback riding—by my dad, my brother Puncher, my sister and me—to keep track of things. We had a large number of horses, which we kept broke up into a bunch for riding, a group of work horses, and some for breeding.

The riding horses and the plow horses were easy to keep track of, but our stud ran wild with his mares and was often found with the wild horses that ran on Redondo Peak and into the Valle Grande. It was a chore to cut out our own, but sometimes we were able to get an unbranded colt, or retrieve horses that belonged to our neighbors. We "broke" the wild horses we caught and usually sold them. There are still several old-timers around who rode after the wild ones. It was a fast and very dangerous chase, more hair-raising than any roller-coaster ride. There were several bands on the Baca Location, the largest thought to be 50 head. The wild horses were cleaned out of the Baca Ranch in the 1930s, and the best of tight fences were installed by Roger Hill and some of his boys.

Every ranch had a couple of big mean dogs to help handle livestock. We had two: A part chow that bit everyone, and a female German Shepherd. They were good at cattle handling; you could put them on a cow in the brush and they would soon have her in the herd. We punished our dogs for running deer, but this female German Shepherd could not resist. Once the dogs jumped out after a spotted fawn they found, chased it, and caught it. My brother was there, and whipped the dogs away with his rope and picked up the exhausted fawn.

It seemed unhurt except for a flap of skin on the hind leg that was bleeding and dirty. Herb thought the wound should be treated, so he brought the little doe home, and we sewed up the flap and put hydrogen peroxide on the wound. We decided that the mother would never find the fawn. Even if we took it back to the general area, the fawn would starve. So it was decided to keep her until she could fend for herself.

We had some goats, so we picked a nanny with lots of milk and taught the fawn to nurse from the surrogate mother. We named her Daisy. In a short while, Daisy thought she was a goat and the goats thought she was one of them. Each day as we turned them out on the hillside, the nannies took their kids and Daisy out to graze. If the goats were stalked by a bobcat or a coyote, they would stampede to the barn and the protection of the ranch dogs and our .30-30 rifle. As Daisy matured, she grew bigger than the goats and always led them to the barn in her 20-foot bounds. She was a pleasure to see and to pet. Of course it was illegal, even then, to keep a deer, but no one ever said anything.

The female German Shepherd did chase another deer during a cattle drive we had on Thompson Ridge. The dogs, after a long chase, brought an old doe and put her in with the herd of cows where she was now safe. We punished the dogs, and the female was later "put down." We got a replacement, and these two never ran deer again.

Just as Daisy reached full size, she and the goats were weaving in and out of the horses as we fed oat hay from the stack. The goats were resented by the horses and cows and were real pests at feeding time. A big old work horse kicked Daisy and killed her dead with one blow. We were all so sad, and she was buried on the hill above the house. We loved her and missed her. She was a true Daisy.

This story appeared in the Jemez Thunder, *May 1, 1999.*

◀▶ DOLLY'S FAMILY ◀▶

Dolly was a snow-white work horse that got off to a bad start. She was a Cochiti Indian horse and had been taught to ride. Her first colt was locked up while a young Indian went visiting. Dolly whinnied for her colt and ran away and threw the Indian rider off. He became entangled in his rope, and when Dolly returned for her colt, the Indian had been dragged to death.

My father went to the funeral. Of course, the Indian family was devastated by this tragedy and sold the horse to my father for a token amount of money. They kept the colt. The horse was used to Indian dialogue, but she learned our language real soon. She was okay to ride, but she was really a work horse, and my father taught her to respond to the old-fashioned "gee" and "haw," which meant to turn to the right or left by a voice command at a distance. She skidded our logs for the winter while someone walked along at the end of the log with no reins. She was put in harness with Star, a black gelding, an unusual team but well-suited to wagons and plows. They pulled our wagon to Albuquerque many times over the years, a three-day trip each way.

If you have read the story titled "Horses Can See in the Dark," you will know about her. We had her for about 20 years, and she bore us about 15 colts in that time. I cannot remember her not being pregnant. She still ran away to join a band of wild horses, but she was easy to catch and drive home after a short run. She usually had a new-born colt at her side. When the crops were in, we let her go all summer.

Her first colt was the only white horse she bore for us. His name was Joker, and he became mine. He was a pet and never offered to buck. We used him for 20 years and finally sold him to Mack Fenton as a "timber cruiser." We were all riding mustangs that were young and rowdy and knew the steep hills and rocky paths that the bands of wild horses used. We could catch and tame them.

The rest of the horses Dolly bore were of all colors. Two were black and we believe they were brothers. One was Dot, my sister's horse, and Zip, a wild one. We imported a big bull who, with no provocation, disemboweled my sister's horse with his long horns. The horse had to be put down. After 60 years, it still brings tears to my sister's eyes that her favorite horse was killed. Zip ran away with me and burst into a clump of trees and knocked himself silly and dislocated my jaw. There was Beauty, a nice sorrel, and a brown horse called Babe, the only two mares she had. All the rest were males, and we made geldings out of them, except for a huge stud we kept who was so mean that he was not afraid of a man or of the geldings. If a fertile mare was nearby, he could kill you.

We traded a lot of horses and had 20 or 30 on hand most of the time. Dolly's colts were no exception. Once she was bred to a Morgan horse who was a giant. By himself he pulled the pickup out of a swollen river with ten 20-pound hogs in the back. He was black and very gentle.

That was Dolly's family, which really put us in the horse business!

This story appeared in the Jemez Thunder *July 15, 2001.*

◄►LAST WOLF IN THE JEMEZ◄►

During the summer of 1937, we became aware that a wolf was in the country. We had seen the tracks, as had others who knew a wolf track from a dog track. Once, when I went to bring in some calves from the lower pasture, I saw a wolf attacking the smaller calves. I thought it might be a dog, but when I shouted, it just looked at me and ran into the brush. It was not a dog!

We kept the calves closer that summer and waited. My father saw more wolf tracks, and eventually saw the wolf. He rode his horse into a campground and saw the wolf eating out of the tin cans and refuse from the camp. He was unarmed at the time, but put his horse right up to the wolf. The wolf growled at the horse, but sensed a man aboard and backed away and ran.

Later that summer we heard a wolf howl at night, and it drove the dogs wild. We had a little flock of sheep that we kept in the corral at night and would let them out in the pasture in the daytime. The leader of the group was an old and wise ewe who wore a loud bell on a leather strap around her neck. If she were molested by coyotes or a bobcat, she led her group to the corral where the dogs and people gave them protection.

One night she failed to bring the sheep in, and we knew there was an emergency! Next morning as we were milking, she came pounding down the road with the bell clanging. We knew she was being chased by some animal, so I grabbed a pistol off the saddle and went to meet her. She was wild-eyed and ran for the barn.

I ran up the canyon where she had come from and found a dead sheep. As I continued up the canyon, I found more sheep until all 11 head were accounted for. For some reason, the wolf had stopped at one of the first killed and was having a feast. I was so excited and out of breath that my pistol wobbled and, of course, I never hit him. He ran into the brush as the six shots scared him. He had broken the sheeps' necks one by one as they tried to get away. The only reason he didn't get the old ewe was the thick strap and clanging bell she wore.

Later that summer, as we were doing the evening chores, my father looked up the hill and saw this wolf. He sent me to the house to get the .30-30 rifle, and the wolf stood still while he took a shot at it. We all agreed that he hit him, although the distance was so far away. We wanted to run up the hill and get the wolf, but we had milk cows in the barn, and my father said the wolf would still be there.

We went up just before dark, and the wolf was gone. We never found him, but a deer hunter that was staying with us said he found him about a half-mile away. He had gone that far before he died. This, we believed, was the last of the wolves in New Mexico and certainly the last of those in the Jemez Mountains.

This story appeared in the Jemez Thunder, *August 1, 2000.*

◄►PET THE COW ◄►

We lived in the city one winter, as the children in our family were getting too advanced in grade school to be home-taught by my mother, who had only a high school education. She insisted that we should learn the rules of regular schools and any things we missed.

We were not used to other kids, and we never knew any of their games, such as football or basketball or even baseball. My father was reluctant to leave the ranch, and he thought a sixth grade education was good enough to handle livestock and run a ranch. We were not in any hurry, so we came in weeks late to school and impatiently left a few weeks before school was out. We were not used to the traffic and electric lights and a lot of things we saw. However, we mixed with our neighbors and had much fun because there were no chores to do, and we could play all we wanted. These town kids had fun. The school work was a little strange, but my mother had taught us all the basics, and some of us excelled in reading and math.

Before leaving the ranch, the family of six felt we had to have a cow for our dairy products. We picked a small Jersey cow that somehow seemed to like people. We could pet her, and she would follow us around to be petted. She was "fresh," and gave the richest of milk, a couple of gallons a day. We rented a house at 725 S. Arno in Albuquerque, and in those days you could have a cow as well as chickens. We converted our garage to a milk shed and built a small corral and chicken pen out back.

When we moved, we had a good farm truck. So we caught Pet, which really was the cow's name, and put a halter on her and led her up the road to a place where we had backed the truck up to a cutbank and led her aboard. As we proceeded the 75 miles to town, we stopped often to see if she was okay. She put her head over the side like a big old dog, and enjoyed every minute of the trip. When we reached our house on Arno, it had a big back porch, and she walked out of the truck and down the three steps and into her new home. She was comfortable in her new pen, but she liked us to come and pet her. She bawled for a visit, and it took a while to learn that she bawled each time the truck came and went. We drank her good milk, and Mr. Lewis, the Jemez Springs ranger, lived across the street, and we sold them fresh milk. They were there for the school and were more or less our age.

One time my father said, "Pet loves that truck, so let's give her a ride." We led her up the porch, and she jumped right into the truck. We were talking about a three-acre ranch on Guadalupe Trail out near Rio Grande Boulevard, so we drove out to see it. Twice we took her to the place that we might buy for the next school year. Once my brother and I insisted that we take her to the zoo. She was as fascinated as the boys, and we all enjoyed the trip.

73

We completed our school and left a few weeks early and took our laying hens and our Pet back to the ranch. That summer a man came to buy a milk cow and picked Pet out of the herd we had. My father put a big price on her but the man paid. We loaded her again in our truck and took her to her new home. We never saw her again, but we wished her well and hoped she would be petted by her new family.

We bought the three acres in north Albuquerque. We drove 12 cows down the 75 miles to Guadalupe Trail and started a little dairy. As we sat and milked these cows, we sometimes talked of Pet, the little cow that loved us—and especially the truck.

This story appeared in the Jemez Thunder, *December 1, 2000.*

◄►JEMEZ MOUNTAINS MUSTANGS◄►

Ever since the old-timers could remember, there were bands of wild horses on the Baca Location. We sometimes caught them for our own use, and very often our domestic horses would run away and join the wild bunch. There were several bands near the Guadalupe, near Stable Mesa and Virgin Canyon, often chased and trapped by the Heath boys, led by Mike Heath.

But our concern was the wild horses on the Baca Ranch. Some of us rode horses that were once wild and now ridden when we chased their own group. They were well fed and knew where the wild ones would run and hide. We were the only ones to capture a few horses, and be paid for separating and returning horses that had joined the wild bunch. The owners were glad to get them back. Sometimes our good studs would acquire a few mares, producing good colts. The Baca was getting more and more mustangs and, though they usually ran in bands of about 15, there was a time when I saw about 45 head at one time. Several bands were probably mixed.

In the 1930s, a man named John Davenport was the honcho for the Baca Ranch. He was called Juan Largo because he was so tall and large, and he had decided to rid the Baca of wild horses. He rebuilt all the fences around the Baca, got rid of the sheep, and stocked it with good beef cattle. He hired Alex, a cowboy, to maintain the fences. When Juan Largo decided to get rid of the wild horses, he hired all the riders he could find, including the Abousleman boys. They rounded up all the horses they could, both wild and domestic, and any rancher who had a horse in there could claim him for $3. Any un-branded horse could be yours for $2.

There were a certain amount of horses that they could not catch or corral, but with tight fences and many riders, they were able to chase the remainder into a dead canyon. The riders, who carried .30-30 rifles and had shot some of the cantankerous mustangs, now proceeded to kill all those horses. For years, the unfortunate horse bones littered the canyon where they were killed. Only a few of us knew where this place was, and none of us spoke of it. Now there are only branded and domestic horses, and very few of them are on the Baca. They raise cattle, and the place is patrolled by four-wheel drive. Locked metal gates control the entrances. The money crop is in the elk that the (guided) hunters can kill with bows and arrows, black powder, and Magnum rifles. There are thousands of elk on the Baca Ranch, but no one owns them. They are wild animals and belong to the general public.

This story appeared in the Jemez Thunder, *May 1, 2000.*

◄► MIKE'S BEAR ◄►

Mike Heath lived at La Cueva and was a logger most of the time, but in the off season he was a hunter and trapper of bobcats and coyotes. He didn't have any livestock or dogs since he was away a lot. Just a little flock of chickens that kept him in eggs.

One summer night he awoke to the squawking of the chickens, and believed someone was raiding his henhouse. He grabbed his shotgun and ran to save his chickens. The door to the henhouse lay flat on the ground. Mike knew right away it must have been a bear.

Mike propped the door back up with an old piece of steam pipe and went back to bed. The next morning he went out to fix the door and saw big bear tracks all around. It was pretty obvious that the bear had stood on his hind legs and hooked his claws over the top of the door and just ripped it down and out, pulling off the heavy hinges and big hasp. Mike repaired the door and nailed cleats so the steam pipe could be propped against the door and the other end braced into a reinforced hole in the ground. Mike checked the henhouse the next morning and nothing was disturbed. However, a few days later he found the door flat on the ground again and more chickens missing.

This was a challenge to Mike. He repaired the door with a few nails and sat up all night with his .30-30 rifle to kill that durned bear. Anyone can guess that the bear didn't show up. Mike decided to sit up another night, but by 3 a.m. the bear didn't show so Mike went to bed. The next morning the door was on the ground, and another chicken was missing.

Now Mike was real mad and had a new plan. He would park his pickup a short distance away facing the henhouse door. Now he could sit in the truck, pull on the headlights, jump out and blaze away when the bear showed up. Of course, the bear never came that night.

Mike slept most of the day, ready to spend another night in the truck cab. Around midnight, he thought he heard something. He sensed the bear was near. He put his hand on the light switch, his rifle on his lap, and the cab door partly open. He heard the clickety-clack on the passenger side of the cab, and turning his head, saw a big old bear peeking in the window at him. Mike jerked on the lights and jumped out ready to shoot, but the bear ran away in the dark behind the pickup. All was not lost, though, as Mike knew the bear would never go near the truck as there might be a man sitting in it with a gun. So he parked the pickup near the henhouse, and the bear never came near.

One night Mike stopped at the Los Ojos bar for a beer and told the boys about his enemy, the bear. They bought another round or two and advised Mike to get home before the bear stole the rest of his chickens. But Mike knew the bear never came until midnight or later. When Mike got home around 10 p.m., the henhouse lay flat on the ground and all the chickens were gone but one old Plymouth Rock hen. Mike was not about to share his last chicken with that dirty old bear, so he wrung the chicken's neck and ate her the next day. Mike saw the bear tracks around the house, checking to see if Mike would get any more chickens.

Some of the people saw this big old cinnamon bear in their headlights at night. About this time, the Forest Service and the campground workers between Battleship Rock and Spence Hot Springs complained that a bear was scattering the garbage cans all over the picnic grounds.

Now a Dr. Hibbins, who was a professor at UNM, heard about this bear. He loved to hunt with hounds. So he made up a hunt with Emmitt Smith from over on the Piñas Negras, who had some bear dogs. They met at La Cueva one Sunday night and worked their way down the river, when the dogs smelled the bear at Spence Springs. Emmitt turned the dogs loose and the chase was on. Fat old Mr. Cinnamon didn't run far before he climbed a tree. Emmitt and the doctor came up and the doctor brought down the bear with his big lever action gun. Mike was none too pleased to hear a town dude had shot his bear. It was not bear season, but no one ever said anything. Dr. Hibbins had the hide tanned and it lies on his study floor. Mike and the bear were both losers.

This story appeared in the Jemez Thunder, *April 1, 1999.*

◄►MIKE THE TRAPPER◄►

A couple of years ago, I wrote about Mike Heath and the predicament he was in with the big old bear that tore down his chicken house and stole his laying hens one by one. Mike could not catch the bear, but a "dude" from Albuquerque hunted him down with hounds.

Mike was a good logger, and he and his wife Wilma, were both full of energy and were able to own their own place in Cañon, near Gilman. Wilma furnished lunches for a few years for the movie stars and extras that were filming around the Jemez area. Mike worked in the log woods, and eventually, he converted World War II surplus trucks and used them to bring the logs out of the woods.

He was finally able to own a new sedan, with a radio and heater, and he was very proud of it. As he was doing his daily routine, he would check his traps that were set along the road down through the canyon. One day in the winter time, he saw some tracks. He stopped the car in the road and got out, and sure enough, there was a bobcat in one of his traps. The bobcat was very much alive and plenty mad and aggressive.

78

Now what to do! Mike had caught coyotes in his traps before. He would find a dead limb about the size of a small baseball bat and hit the coyote between the ears, and that subdued him. So Mike thought about that, found a good pitch limb, and gave the bobcat a hard hit. Thinking it was dead, he picked up the cat and the trap and threw them both in the back of his new sedan. He started the engine and was calculating the worth of his good fortune, this huge cat and his winter fur.

In a few minutes, the cat came alive, and there was no room for both of them in the car. There was nothing else for Mike to do as this wild cat bounced all around, so he opened the door and jumped out, the bobcat right behind him. Mike being a little dazed from the tumble, climbed back up to the road and found the car gone! From all the turmoil, it had slipped into gear and had gone down the road another 100 yards and hit a tree before it stopped. Of course, the bobcat got away. So much for his trapping days!

Mike and Wilma were the "characters" of Jemez Springs. They are both gone now, but their second and third generations still live in the area. Exciting times!

This story appeared in the Jemez Thunder, *December 15, 2001.*

◄►SAGA OF MONTROSE THE COW◄►

We had a string of milk cows, and we always tried to improve our herd. Once in Albuquerque, we talked to a Mr. Bezmeich who was the owner of the biggest dairy around Albuquerque. His place was near Indian School Road and Fourth Street. He was the mayor of the town at that time and always hunted out of our ranch for deer and turkey. He had a giant Holstein cow that gave five gallons of milk twice a day. Her bag was five-gallon size and the udders were thicker than the milkers could grasp. Mr. Bezmeich had a hard time as there were no milking machines at the time. My dad bought this cow cheap and brought this big Holstein home, and we named her Montrose.

We could only milk her by a relay between my dad and my brother, and we could not believe the ten gallons of milk she gave every day. Our goal was for her to give us a heifer or two to improve our herd. We kept her and babied her, and she was a gentle old thing. But the first calf she had was a bull. We kept her until she had another, and it also was a bull. Over a period of years she finally had a heifer calf. We were over-joyed as the calf was another giant and looked just like her. We were proud to show off our new Holstein. We let the new calf drink most of the mother's milk, and she was a beautiful thing.

When she was well-grown and was being weaned, she was a pet but still wanted to be near her mother. We kept her separated, and it was a chore to keep her locked up in the calf pen. One fall day, as I tried to pen her up, she ran past me for the third time. I picked up a rock the size of a hen egg and threw it at her. It hit her between the eyes and she fell dead. We could not believe she would die, but she never regained con-sciousness. There was nothing to do but butcher her. This was at a time when we were harvesting the crops, and we had field hands to eat with us. They had never tasted such wonderful veal. But most of us could not eat her meat, especially me, as I can still remember the accident that killed her.

My father decided this was the end of Montrose. She was bad luck. She was fresh and would bring a lot at the sales ring, but we were tired of milking her, and the next calf would proba-bly be another bull. So we loaded her in the pickup, and my dad started for town. In a couple of hours my dad came back up the road on foot, leading Montrose. We thought the pickup had stalled, but it was even worse—a wreck. The rain slick caused my dad to meet an empty log truck on his side of the road head on. Montrose came through the back window of the truck, bringing most of the cab with her. It was hard to get her and my dad out, but they were only skinned up and bloodied.

My dad healed up, and we got a new pickup. My dad was determined to sell her this time. She was gone. My dad never forgave me for throwing that rock, nor did I forgive myself.

This story appeared in the Jemez Thunder, *June 15, 2000.*

◄►HORSES IN THE BIG LOG WOODS◄►

Teams of horses were just as important as the men when they began to cut the timber in the Jemez Mountains. When the logs were felled, a team was used to "snake" the logs through the forest where they could be loaded on a train and later loaded onto a truck. The trees were usually cut in 30-foot lengths, and each section had to be pulled out to a level place to be taken away. Sometimes it was uphill and very often on a side hill where the rolling log could be a real danger to the driver and the horses, especially if the ground was wet or covered with snow. Logs were brought down the mountains by these well-trained horses. The horses used a cutaway lane called a skid trail. It could not be too steep, as the logs must not catch up to the team, but with enough downhill pitch so that the team could easily pull the load.

The place where the train stopped was called a landing, and the loggers had names such as O'Neal for them. These log horses were a lot bigger than the usual teams in the mountains. They did heavy work from daylight to dusk and usually weighed 2,000 pounds apiece. They were pets for the drivers and had to have new shoes quite often. They must be fed grain and hay each day and were expensive. The ranchers used smaller teams to pull their wagons and walking plows. Horses used for logging were Belgians, Percherons or Clydesdales, mixed with a smaller horse. They were trained to hear the driver's voice and the words "gee" and "haw." "Gee" meant turn to the right and "haw" to the left. The driver could walk along next to the team and guide them without lines which were neatly tied to the hames near the collar. They also understood "whoa," "giddup," and "backup."

When a team pulled a log to the beginning of a skid trail, the horses and logs were sent down by themselves. When the horses that pulled the logs reached the bottom at the landing, they were unhooked and sent back up the hill for another log. These trails could be a mile long, and the horses went up and down themselves. If the log hit a stump or became entangled, the horse stood still until someone came to help. When they reached the bottom and a place was clear, the log was put in place. At the top, they came and stood in front of the log. These skid trails can still be seen today.

The horses were like the men who spent their life in the woods. Some lived to a ripe old age, but most wore out early and usually were crippled in accidents. This is a tribute to the horses' intelligence and labor. By World War II, caterpillars and trucks could reach the top of the mountains, and horses were not used again.

This story appeared in the Jemez Thunder, *September 15, 2000.*

MOUNTAIN TRAVEL

Bettie, Dorothy, Joe, Herb and Art Routledge go to the Presbyterian Church in Jemez Springs in their new Ford. 1926

◄►BLAZING TRAILS◄►

In the 1800s, there was a big fort between Las Vegas, New Mexico and Santa Fe. My grandfather, who had a business in Glorieta, supplied the fort with all kinds of merchandise, but specialized in lumber from his sawmill. Pack animals and wagons came from the fort on the way to Fort Wingate and then on to Prescott and Yuma, Arizona. It was a complex network of roads and horseback travel.

For the Cavalry and pack animals, there were a lot of horse trails that went through the Jemez area to reach Cuba on the way to Fort Wingate and Prescott. The Jemez Mountains were very hard to get through, even by horseback, all the way from Española to Cuba. Riders on horseback carrying hatchets marked the trails on the trunks of trees every so often so that the next person might find his way. The trees were marked at about seven feet so that the man with the hatchet could chip some bark two inches wide and five inches long from the tree without dismounting. These were called blazes. If there was a branch on the trail it would be marked by a different sign. Sometimes two blazes and a small cut underneath.

The blazed trail went from Española through the mountains until it reached Sulphur Springs, our ranch and Thompson Ridge, then crossed the San Antonio River and came out at Fenton's place. From there, it went to Peñas Negras and finally Cuba. The wagon roads went much farther and could not go into the timber and steep climbs. They were easy to follow, as the wagon ruts showed the way. The wagon road went from the fort to Taos and into Chama.

A more direct route to Cuba was through the Valles Caldera, at that time called the Baca Location. The ground was more level for the wagons north of the horse trails. There was a cut in the mountains and the road came out at the Seven Springs Fish Hatchery. Then, they went down the river and climbed out to join the horse trails at Rio de las Vacas and on to Cuba, a distance of about 55 miles by horseback from Sulphur Springs.

The rest was easy to follow as it was more like desert, and the old wheel ruts are still there down Canyon Largo and on to Fort Wingate. Some of the old blazes can still be found on some of the old trees, but the pathway and old trails are gone.

This story appeared in the Jemez Thunder, *June 1, 2002.*

◄►BRIDGES OF SANDOVAL COUNTY◄►

There were practically no bridges in Sandoval County in the old days.

If your wagon was parked at J. Korber's Warehouse in Albuquerque and you headed home for the Jemez, you could cross the Rio Grande just south of Corrales on a narrow and rickety one-way bridge, or go to Bernalillo where there was a wooden one-way bridge. I once saw this bridge with a foot of water running over the floor when the Rio Grande was at flood stage. Everyone was afraid to cross until the water went down and we could see if the floor was still there. From there on, there were no bridges at all.

As you headed north and might want to stop at Zia or Santa Ana, you had to ford the Jemez River at each pueblo. There were many arroyos along this stretch, and you never crossed one before you looked up toward the source to see if a wall of water was coming down to wash you away. People had drowned at these crossings as wagons, and later cars, were washed away.

There was a ford across the Rio Salado south of San Ysidro and another just north of San Ysidro as you crossed the Jemez to the pueblo. The road went right through the pueblo all the way, turned hard right, and then left to cross the Rio Chacita. This is the place in 1928 where we arrived just in time to see a car being swept away by a cloudburst that came down at Ponderosa. The couple in the car was able to swim ashore down river. The next ford was at Cañon if you were going up the Guadalupe toward the Rio de las Vacas. We stayed on the east side of the Jemez all the way to Soda Dam. Here was the most dangerous ford of all, with steep banks, swift water and a boulder-covered bottom —bad in dry weather and a no-no in flood stage.

One time we arrived there when the Jemez was flooding, and our neighbor, Tim Hofheins, was stopped there, too. My dad and Tim figured they could combine the two teams and would be able to take one wagon across at a time. My father drove and the wagon got hung up in the boulders. Now the two teams tangled and went down in the swift water. Dad grabbed the axe and cut the tongue out of the wagon to release the horses, but Tim's team drowned. They were able to salvage the wagon and get across the next day with a replacement team.

The road stayed on the west side of the river, and past Battleship Rock it stayed in the very bottom of the canyon where it was so rough and rocky, a single team could hardly pull a heavy wagon.

At La Cueva, we forded the San Antonio just above where the Sulphur and the Redondo came in to form the Jemez. If you were going to see the Hofheinses or the Maestases, you would

86

have to ford the San Antonio again, as they were all across the river, as was the road to Fenton's ranch. Continuing up the canyon (Route 4), if you were going towards Los Alamos, you had to ford the Redondo here and farther on at the falls. If you continued up Sulphur Canyon, you would ford Sulphur Creek and Freelove to be at our ranch. If you went on to Sulphurs, you would ford the creek four more times.

While these crossings gave your horses a chance to drink, they were sometimes dangerous. If you happened to be afoot, you could get your shoes wet unless you took them off or found a fallen tree trunk to cross on. It did help to keep the wagon wheels from drying out. In 1925, 1928 and 1939, we began to get bridges, one by one. Now as I whiz along the paved roads and cross the fine concrete bridges, each one recalls the days when it was different.

This story appeared in the Jemez Thunder, *March 1, 1999.*

◄►ROUGH ROAD TO JEMEZ GETS PAVED◄►

The steep, rocky wagon road to Jemez Springs and the high country above it that wore out teams and mankind finally got a road crew in 1925. That made it possible for autos to climb up the mountain. Jemez Springs could be reached by a strong car before 1925, but that was the end of the road. A "pick and shovel" gang using some horses and TNT powder in kegs, along with a water-boy (who happened to be my cousin), came in 1925.

This gang hacked out a one-way road up the canyon, and at Battleship Rock they took to the west side of the river and left the bottom. A one-way cut was made in the clay bank all the way to La Cueva, about where the present road is now. Here the road forked, and with a series of switchbacks, climbed the Fenton mountain and into the Cebolla (now Highway 126).

The other fork went up Sulphur Canyon and hit a dead end at Sulphur Springs. In 1927, the road crew of about 50 men came back, and this time they had a small Caterpillar, a road grader, and a good supply of dynamite. This crew widened the road and smoothed it. Most of the ranchers bought their first cars.

In 1933 and 1934, the CCC came. They built new roads, one from Fenton to Cuba, and another through the mountains to Española, via Los Alamos (Highway 4). They also built the road from upper Vallecitos to lower Vallecitos via Paliza and Ponderosa (Highway 290). They also built a new road that branched off from Highway 4 and went down to Cochiti and Algodones via the old mining town of Bland. By 1936, there was a paved road that reached San Ysidro, this by a contractor named Jim Kisam. A year later they paved the road on up to Cuba and Jemez Springs.

This called for a real celebration at Jemez Springs, and a banner was put across the street at the Los Ojos bar proclaiming "Albuquerque One Hour Away!!!" I think Freddy Abousleman was the only one who could make it either way in one hour. He had a new Hudson Terraplane coupé, with a small pickup box on the back instead of a trunk and lid. The Terraplane could hit 90 mph. The rest of our old pickups labored at about 50 on the crooked two-lane blacktop.

The celebration at Jemez Springs lasted three days of dancing and socializing, and included a rodeo in Abousleman's alfalfa field. The Routledges furnished the rodeo stock and some of the riders. We had a judge's stand, and everyone wanted to be up there. A volunteer crew started a fight over this, and it became the main activity for three days. We had brought in a deputy sheriff from Bernalillo to keep order, which was a hopeless job. The mountain people, now full of strong drink, accused the deputy of hiding behind his gun and badge. So he

88

took them off and lay them on top of his patrol car, and went to "fist city" with Mike Heath, the best rough and tumble man around. Mike was just a little drunk and didn't get to hit the deputy, and got beat. The deputy then put his badge and gun back on and locked Mike, Talmidge King, and Arnon Crandell (who got hit in his one good eye) in a nearby cellar until they sobered up. The deputy was quite a man. Some time later, as he patrolled a dance at Bernalillo, he was jumped by a gang, some of them his cousins, and killed with his own gun.

The Jemez Fiesta did last three days, and it was enough for all of us. Some took home some bad cuts and bruises; one man went home without his left ear, which I saw bitten off clean and spit in the alfalfa field. Most had headaches, but there was a lot of fun and some romance. The mountain people had quite a time.

Each time I come back to Jemez, I see these good paved roads and bridges and the local law harvesting the tourists through MVD laws and speed traps. At least we were spared this. The old log roads opened up the high country to the four-wheelers and to the places we used to run cattle and hunt on foot. Unless you can afford a permit on the Baca, these things are only history.

This story appeared in the Jemez Thunder, *February 1, 2000.*

◀▶ WHEN WE TRADED WAGONS FOR CARS ◀▶

In 1925, they began to build roads into the Jemez Mountains. A good car could reach Jemez Springs, and an even better one could go as far as Battleship Rock. After Battleship Rock, the wagon road took to the bottom of the Jemez River and it was difficult for a good team to reach La Cueva. The pick and shovel gang, the horses and the blasting powder, built above the river bottom on the left side and carved the road up above the bank where the dirt was softer. It took a lot of dirt moving and tree cutting, and much of the road was one way only, wide enough for a 10-foot car. If you should happen to meet someone, you would have to back up until you could pass, usually it was the down-coming car: The upcoming car was having enough trouble as it was.

The first car we ever saw belonged to Diego Baca, who was a big sheep rancher, but had little to do with the Baca Location. He drove a Lincoln with a four-speed transmission, and it was something to see when it pulled into the ranch, proving it could be done. It set my father to thinking. If we got one, a trip to town would only be a day each way, and a trip to Jemez for mail would take less than a day. The next time my father went to Bernalillo, he stopped at the Ford garage to see if we could afford one. There was a Chevrolet dealership owned by a Mr. Caldwell. My father took the Ford, as it seemed to have less gears, and the Ford cost less. He picked a Touring with a Ruestal in it for mountain driving. My father didn't know how to drive it and could not take it home.

What about the team and wagon? So Mr. Quickie, who was the garage owner, said he would deliver it to our ranch next Tuesday. We were all so happy to know we would be riding in an automobile. Sure enough, about noon, after a 14-hour trip, the new touring car arrived, followed by a new Lincoln driven by Mr. Quickie. The chief mechanic drove the touring car. We had dinner, and after dinner the mechanic took my father to a lower field and taught him to drive. He also taught him how to start the car and change a tire. They soon left, as it was 12 hours to Bernalillo. We were so proud of it, and we each looked to see if it was still there. We had decided to wait for Sunday, and we would ride down to Jemez Springs, get the mail, and my mother could put us in a real church.

We all dressed up and rolled the car out of the barn. My father cranked it and it would not start. He cranked it until his gloves were worn out and he was nearly dead from upset and frustration. We rolled it back in the barn, and we were all downhearted. My father sent word to Mr. Quickie to come and get it, and to bring our money. Two days' later Mr. Quickie showed up at noon. The mechanic went to the Ford and lifted the hood and saw at once what the trouble was. The choke was disconnected and had lost a pin on the road, a small cotter pin was all it needed. The car started the first crank. Once we had dinner and Mr. Quickie smoothed my father's feathers, they returned to town and we didn't have much trouble with it. We had to store it in the winter because of the snow and cold, but for a little while, we had the only car in the mountains.

Today we never see a car delivered 14 hours away and have the dealership come to see about it if there is trouble. Those were the days when there was salesmanship and concern for the people that bought it.

This story appeared in the Jemez Thunder, *July 15, 1999.*

◄►WATER FOR OUR RADIATORS◄►

In the early days when we drove Model T Fords, you always kept a lookout for places you could get water for your radiators. Between Bernalillo and San Ysidro, there was no water, and you had to carry some with you across the barren land. For people who could afford a kit, they bought a compact bundle that fastened to the running board. There was a white can for water, a blue can for oil, and a red can for gasoline. Each one held a gallon. All of us who could not buy this kit made up our own. We used a coal oil can for gas, and a five-gallon can for water, and put oil in still another can.

To those of us who lived in La Cueva, the first stop out of Bernalillo was San Ysidro, where the teams had watered for many years, as there was a windmill. We filled our radiator and replenished our water can. We could also get water from the Jemez River, but sometimes you had to walk a little. As the old road followed up the canyon, there was some low gear driving, and the Model T would really heat up in the summertime.

The radiators were made of brass and copper and could use any kind of water, and the big honeycombs could tolerate a lot of muddy water, too. If a stone punctured the radiator, you could pinch off the injury, or you might seal it with chewing gum. We found out that Bull Durham tobacco was a good radiator sealant, but sawdust would stop it up, too.

As you left Jemez Springs, the road became steeper, and at 9,000 feet, water boiled at 190 degrees instead of 212. If you needed water from Battleship Rock to La Cueva, it was a long way down. Just before you reached La Cueva, there was a place called The Cold Spring that emerged at 45 degrees. It chilled your teeth and there was a good flow. If you went on to Fenton's, there was Horseshoe Springs part way up, and there was another part way up on the other side.

Water was important to the motorist, but when winter came, we had to drain the engine every night or suffer a broken block. We tried not to use the cars in winter because so much happened, like the gas we used sometimes had water in it, and the gas line would freeze, or the radiator could freeze even with the engine running. The brakes would freeze and the springs would break at 20 below. I remember when we drained radiators how we hated to lie on our backs and let the water run down our sleeves. Later, you had to lie down to replace the petcock or valve, and refill with cold water, and then you probably couldn't start the car anyway. Until 1936, we had no Prestone (or glycol) coolant, and then when antifreeze came along it was too expensive to use because of World War II. We tried alcohol, but it was not a good coolant and sometimes caught fire.

Now we use coolant summer and winter, and it only has to be changed every couple of years. And now they are coming up with a solution that will last the life of the car—providing it does not leak out. We have come a long way: no radiators to fill, and with fuel injection the car will even start in sub-zero weather!

This story appeared in the Jemez Thunder, *June 1, 2000.*

◄►WHEN RAILROADS CAME TO THE JEMEZ◄►

In the 1920s, when they began to log the Jemez country, a railroad came in to haul the logs to Bernalillo to be sawed into lumber. The railroad followed the Jemez River most of the way to take advantage of the flat ground near the river. When the rail bed reached Cañon and the Guadalupe, it turned, and went up the river to Gilman. Here was a box canyon with falls that seemed impossible to get by. The railroad built a trestle and blasted the Gilman Tunnels on the upper end and got past this place. They moved a lot of dirt as they made their way upriver to the Cebolla.

At Porter Landing, when the log woods were going good, the bunk houses were full and the mess hall was using a cow or steer once a week. Mr. McCoy was the head cook there, and he was called The Real McCoy! Our ranch furnished the beef and delivered it once a week, along with some dairy products. There were times when we cleaned out the mess hall and had dances there, but the lumberjacks were prone to fight among

93

themselves (lack of women) and with the outsiders, so we passed up most of them.

I can remember ordering a wagon and having it delivered by train to Porter Landing. It came with the wheels separate, and the axles as well as the tongue. The tools to assemble it came crated, and it had to be built right there.

The railroad had an eight-passenger Packard sedan that was fitted with train wheels and was their courier to Bernalillo for mail and emergencies, and ran between trains. The pilot set the hand throttle on 35 miles per hour and read a book while he made the trip, cautioning any passenger to watch out for cattle on the tracks.

Most of the upper canyons were finally logged out. The line was shortened to Cañon, and trucks were used to haul down the mountains to Cañon. The rails were taken up for steel, and there were many washouts along the way. After the war, Camp Gilman was set up, and a small town appeared, with mess halls and schools. This time we danced in the school house and still fought a little. Gilman was a diesel electric mill, and it ran on electricity. Huge diesel trucks brought the logs from even further up the mountains to Gilman, and other trucks took the lumber to Bernalillo.

The old steam engines are gone, and we seldom meet a log truck that used to scare us so badly when the roads were so narrow and unpaved. But the trains were fun, and somehow thrilled us all.

This story appeared in the Jemez Thunder, *November 15, 1999.*

◀▶A RIDE ON A BALDEY TRUCK◀▶

In the Depression days, the loggers had to use the best tools at the least cost. The New Mexico Lumber and Timber Company bought trucks without cabs. They were called "baldeys" because they had only a hood and front fenders and nothing back of the dash except a frame and wheels like we see at the beginnings of a motor home—but nothing on top. They were rigged to pull trailers that were made from junked front or back ends of old trucks and had single wheels. They were connected by wood poles or pipe to the back of the truck with no cab.

These little trucks were 1½ ton, and there were no trailer brakes. They sometimes hauled up to 10 tons up and down our narrow dirt roads. On the return trip to the woods, they had to drag the trailer, as there was no way to load or carry it on the back of the truck. The only control on these steep roads was by downshifting to low or compound and creep along. If the engine died or a clutch burned out or a driveline broke, you were now on a runaway truck with a load of logs at your shirt collar. Of course, the trucks wore out in a year.

The landing was at Cañon, across the river where the train waited, as it no longer went through the tunnels. A crude one-way bridge made out of logs spanned the river without any railings to keep you up there. At this time, the truck camp was on Redondo Creek near the road to El Cajete, and they were logging Sulphur Canyon and Thompson Ridge. The man in charge of the truck camp was a disgusting old sea captain who ruled with an iron fist. At 4 o'clock every morning, he awoke the entire camp as he yelled at the top of his lungs, "Haul logs or haul ass, you Redondo s.o.b." When it rained, it was impossible with high centers and deep ruts. In fair weather, the dust was so thick you had to stop if a truck passed either way. Now, trucks that belonged to New Mexico Lumber and Timber Company held sway, but those not in their employ were called "gippos" and were operated by individuals or by someone who bought the trucks and hired drivers. They were given so much money for every log they laid down at the Cañon landing.

The poor little trucks were six-cylinder Chevrolets or flathead Fords. They lasted only a year or two, if they were not wrecked. The dealerships said they must be paid for in one year, and there was no insurance, so they were always paying on a truck. The runaways were numerous, and the steep hairpin turns at Spence Hot Springs claimed their share! A runaway truck could be saved if you used small trees to stop it, or it could be run up a bank and turned over on the road. In any event, the driver bailed out, and there were no doors or anything to keep you from jumping out as you sat on a seat on the gas tank. No one seemed to get killed, except one poor fellow who jumped and the trailer ran over him. One unlucky guy at Deer Creek rode his truck all the way to the flats. It ran through the schoolhouse and turned it to splinters. It was unoccupied, but he had to help the town fathers rebuild another school.

In a few years, no more zero mornings and choking dust, as trucks with cabs helped the hardworking drivers. All of us dreaded to meet these trucks, because you could never be sure they were able to stop. If you had to go down the canyon, you fell in behind a loaded truck and ate his dust all the way down.

A return trip was after dark, when the trucks were not running. Even after the big Kenworths with dual axles and dual trailers with power brakes came, we were still glad when all the logs were down, and we did not have to share the road with these runaway trucks!

This story appeared in the Jemez Thunder, *April 1, 2001.*

MOUNTAIN FOLK

Art and Ethel

◄►A CAN OF SARDINES ◄►

In the old days when we planted our crops, we used a hand plow and a team of horses. We had 40 acres to plant in oat hay, and several fields of potatoes and turnips to plant. All of this was an awful lot of work for a man and his two small sons, so we hunted around for a man to help. We found a good one in Jemez Pueblo, and at the time he happened to be the Governor of Jemez Pueblo. He not only owned a team, but was willing to work from daylight to dark for a little bit of cash! His name was George Toledo—very well-known and coveted by the Jemez Indians. He was a graduate of the Indian School in Albuquerque, and he was fluent in English, Spanish and the Jemez Indian language. All of us liked him, and he slept in our upstairs bedroom.

One time when I was chosen to help him cultivate potatoes to keep down the weeds, we used a single horse to pull the walking cultivator. My job was to stay astride of this big work-horse and be sure he stayed in the rows between the potato plants. I was only six or seven years old, and it was a chore to ride the work horse with a harness on and no saddle—only the hame straps and blinders bridle to hang on to. George never said anything to me unless I let the horse wander into the plants.

The days were very long, and in order to keep us in the fields we took lunches, and we ate under a shade tree. We fed the horse a "morale," which was a bag for the oats, and the horse could rest and eat his grain. On this particular day, my mother made lunches, and as a treat she put a can of sardines as well as sandwiches in George's lunch. Oh, how he loved sardines, but they did not do much for me. George peeled back the lid on the can and took out his pocketknife and speared them one

99

at a time and ate them. You could hear him moan in apprecia-
tion for the flavor of the sardines. He ate half of the can and
decided to keep the rest for a treat the next day. He put the
half-filled can up in a fork of a tree. Now, we all know that
you must not let anything remain in a tin can for even a little
while or it will probably kill you.

The next day, we came back to the same shade tree, and
George took down the can of sardines and ate the rest of them.
I was horrified and expected him to keel over right away. We
plowed the rest of the day, and I watched to see if he became
ill. He remained good and healthy and bragged about the flavor of the sardines for several days. I guessed the oil in the
fish kept the can from killing him. This was one tough Governor of Jemez Pueblo!

This story appeared in the Jemez Thunder, *January 15, 2001.*

◀▶ THE WILD MAN OF NEW MEXICO ◀▶

Most of us have heard about Big Foot in Washington or Ore-
gon or Yeti in the Himalayas. We had something like it in the
Jemez Mountains. He had been seen before, but rarely observed. It was in the mining town of Bland, which was in a
deep canyon below Los Alamos, that he was first seen, sitting
high on the bluffs, looking down on the town. My father and
grandfather lived there then. When I began to tell my father
about Big Foot, he told me about the Wild Man, as they called
him then.

This man was not a Big Foot, but appeared to be the regular
size of any man, but we could not see his features. He seemed
to wear clothes of some kind. My grandfather watched him
through field glasses and said he was a hermit of some kind.

But everyone was uneasy about him, and some of the men thought he might come down and molest the women while the men were at work in the mine. Soon, small things were missing, and they blamed the Wild Man, but no one ever saw him and the dogs never barked, nor did they ever see his tracks in the town. Some said that he was around when they went to their outhouses in the middle of the night.

All the talk at the saloons, and the idle talk among the mine laborers, was always of the Wild Man. Finally, some of the town toughs put a gang together to hunt him down. They made several trips up there, but found no sign of him. He sat and watched them get ready to come after him. But one Sunday, they saw him up there, and the town toughs as well as many of the miners, joined in an extensive hunt, with some on horseback, and they even brought along a couple of dogs.

They finally did catch up with him this time and began to shoot at him, and a fatal bullet killed him. When they had a chance to look him over, he was simply a hermit—a man about 50 years old—a tramp in worn clothes. They found a crack in the rocks and dropped him down inside and covered him up with nearby stones. They never did find his hideout, which must have been in one of the caves in the area.

The hunters returned to town, and there was much drinking and talk of what had been done. My grandfather, among others, was outraged that they had killed this man for no reason at all. They had no constable or sheriff then, and my grandfather, Joe, demanded that someone go to Santa Fe and summon the law, and that the shooters be tried for murder. But no one wanted to fetch the law, not even my grandfather. So the talk soon stopped and nothing was said outside of the town. It was not that well known. My people never forgot what happened to a lonely old hermit. The poor old guy looked down on a town that had no compassion for a stranger.

This story appeared in the Jemez Thunder, *February 15, 2000.*

◀▶ JOHN BARLEYCORN ◀▶

Who and what is John Barleycorn? It is one of the old-fashioned names for whiskey. Jack London wrote a book with this title, which is a little hard to find, that covers his enjoyment and addiction to John Barleycorn. I'm sure the Jemez Mountains always had someone making whiskey, but I expect it was of dubious quality. No one cared who made it, especially my family. No one smoked or drank in our clan. It was bad for you! People tended to their own business and left their neighbors alone.

In the '30s, the Linham family came here from Tennessee to work the crops. Pa Linham was one expert with a still, and soon he was making whiskey that the users said was as good as Jack Daniels. The "Pro-Hibs" never bothered him and everyone liked him. Part of his old family caught up with him, and his brother-in-law turned him in for a fee. The feds came and busted up the still, which was in a little canyon inside the edge of the ranch. Mr. Linham got one year in jail and spent it at the Bernalillo Courthouse as cook for the jail and the Sheriff's Department. He bought all the groceries across the street and his cell door was never locked. He came and went as he pleased.

He had three sons and two nice daughters. While Mr. Linham was away, his oldest son, Joe, built a new still in a different place. Joe had bad eyes and today would be declared legally blind. But he had the old man's talent. Joe made good stuff

102

which cost 50 cents a pint, $1 a quart, and $3 per gallon. It was 100 proof, but you could get 200 proof on special order for more money for "White Lightning."

There was a little store in Jemez owned by J. D. Johnston who kept John Barleycorn under the counter for walk-in trade. No one ever bothered J. D., so Joe had a good, safe market. Joe wanted to do better, so he pulled up stakes and moved to Albuquerque. He set up a still in the Manzano Mountains and did very well. He now had a touring car, a driver and a partner, and a burro to pack the whiskey out.

The feds followed the car loaded with supplies out of town and arrested the driver, then followed the burro trail up to the still. Joe and his partner escaped, but the still was demolished. Joe and his partner then leased an old farm on the outskirts of Belen and set up their still in a big old hay barn. Business was good. They bought the sheriff off, so all went well until the still exploded and set the barn on fire. Half the people in Belen showed up to watch it burn. Joe ran one way and his partner the other.

This story appeared in the Jemez Thunder, *March 15, 1999.*

◀▶ THE BEE MAN ◀▶

In the summertime, the Jemez had a preponderance of strangers who came to fish and camp, trade horses, prospect, and just view our lovely country as they took the warm baths in our springs. Many that came through our trails and roads didn't tell us what their business was. We had some characters.

One summer, a man came up from the Rio Grande Valley to supply honey to the Jemez people. He sold comb honey in the little square boxes that came from the hive and that still had the wax in them. It was a treat for us who lived too high for honey bees. He had a good quantity of it, and we all bought this wonderful food. I have forgotten what he charged, and sometimes he would trade it for vegetables, meat and dairy products. He had a new, neat little wagon, with a tent and all the camping utensils. He had a nice gentle team, and another horse tied behind the wagon. He also had a 10-year-old girl, his daughter, with him. They camped and enjoyed the summer in the mountains. We heard his wife was dead. He was a friendly man, and seemed to have a good education. He stayed with us on our property near the house, while he bathed in the waters of Sulphur Springs. The girl was friendly, but my brother and I were not used to strange girls.

As he moved along to a ranch or farm, he pulled a little joke on us all. He took the horse from behind the wagon, exchanging it for one of the team, perhaps smearing a little mud on the horse, and ruffling the mane and tail. As he approached and became acquainted, he asked if my dad had any sporting blood in him. The Bee Man said that he had a plow horse that would outrun most of the cow ponies around, and would my dad like to put a horse up against his plow horse—any horse. The race was a half-mile down the road. He would bet $50 or the winner take both horses. My dad was a horse trader, and saw it was a young horse fitted with track shoes and was off the race track.

When he and the girl left us, we were the best of friends. We had traded spuds and meat and dairy products for his wonderful honey. But we would not race him. He finally moved on to another ranch, and we soon learned he switched the horses and got a bet from the owner. Now the "work horse" was unhitched and a race horse saddle was put on him, and the 10-year-old girl rode him to a "no contest" victory. Most were fooled, and all remembered the deceit and never bit again. He came a second summer to camp at our place, but he was careful to avoid the places where he had won. When he left us, he went over to Cuba, and I am sure he found more places to play his little game. He was always friendly and always seemed to escape any real retribution or pistol shots.

We never ate honey without thinking about The Bee Man and his little daughter.

This story appeared in the Jemez Thunder, September 15, 1999.

◄►HEY, WATER BOY! ◄►

In the old days when everyone was stampeding to the Yukon in Alaska for the gold rush, my father had an aunt named Molly who married a man from Bland. He also went to Alaska, leaving Molly—who by now had three children—behind. The middle child was named Andrew (Cub) Dinsmore who was 13 years old at the time, but who really looked like an adult for his age, short and very husky.

My dad bought 100 goats from a goat herder's estate for a very small price. We had purchased a ranch on Freelove Canyon, and it was my cousin's duty to herd the goats 75 miles to our ranch. It was a three-day trip, but one cannot even imagine the trouble it was to drive those 100 goats 75 miles! Cub had a lot of nerve and would fight a buzz saw. He lived with us for his room and board.

A while later, after they had used some black powder to blast the rocks out of the way, a crew built a road that would accommodate a car down through the canyon. While all this work was going on, they needed a "water boy"—a young person who would bring a pail of water and a dipper for the workers to drink out of. They hired Cub, and he carried a pail of water from our spring and a dipper to every man as he

105

walked back and forth to each worker for 25 cents a day and was very happy to get that! The men hollered "Hey, water boy!" all day long.

Now the road crew needed some trees and asked my dad to furnish a team, which of course he did, but specified that Cub would drive them. The foreman protested that Cub was too young, but my dad held fast as he knew Cub could handle the job very well. My father got paid for the team and the driver got a raise. When they finished building the road and moved away, Cub went with them. He became a teamster and we would only hear from him once in a while. In a few years, he became foreman on this job and part of his duty was to whip each disgruntled worker who challenged him. He did a lot of fighting but had a lot of friends in the highway construction business. He came to see us one time and was driving a brand new car and wanted to go fishing. By now he was completely in charge of the construction company and had paved the road from Albuquerque to Gallup. He was in contact with someone from Los Alamos, and they had a special project for him. They sent him to Alamogordo and at the end of a dirt road he built a huge tower, but no one said what it was for. We all know now that was the first atomic bomb, and "Fat Man" was exploded there. The steel tower disappeared and the sand around the bottom turned to glass. He was amazed to see it, just as I was in later years.

There was no more "Hey, water boy!" A Jemez man made good!

This story appeared in the Jemez Thunder, *February 1, 2001.*

◀▶ GUN FIGHT AT BLAND ◀▶

There was going to be a gun fight sooner or later—the sooner the better! This was on the edge of the Jemez Mountains, and many of the mountain people were involved. Dunsmore rode down from Glorieta and heard that Crandell (the Glorieta blacksmith) had settled in Bland. They had had a misunderstanding that he thought could be settled at once. No one remembers what the "beef" was about, but Dunsmore came down looking for Crandell. Crandell saw the fellow ride in, and he was not about to meet this Mr. Dunsmore without a gun of his own. He stuck the gun on the left side of his belt and proceeded to the bar. Dunsmore always wore a belt with a holster and was said to be a tough nut who sometimes drew on unarmed men.

The two armed men stood at each end of the bar and began to quibble. Now everyone knew what the "beef" was about. The younger fellows wanted to see the fight, so they gathered outside the front door. There was Art Routledge, Tim Hofheins, Talmadge King—not the young Talmadge we knew, but his father—and Miles Bagwell. They were not allowed inside the bar, as they were only 10 or 12 years old at the time, but they wanted to see the fight so they looked under the door. Inside the bar, the argument started to get hot and heavy, and the other patrons decided they had somewhere else to go. These two kept arguing and each had a gun, and people knew someone might get hurt. As they left, they told the kids to go home and stay away.

Now we have to say that hardly anyone really had a chance at gunplay. Shells cost a lot and a month's supply cost a couple of weeks' wages. So most just bought a supply and hardly ever used them, which meant that people weren't very good marksmen, and would hardly ever hit anyone unless they were very close to each other.

As the hot and heavy argument grew to a louder pitch, the bartender stood between the men. All the other patrons had gone, and the kids were still peeking under the door. The men finally drew their guns and blazed away. The guns in those days had six cylinders, but one was kept empty for safety purposes, so they had 10 shots and fired five shots each. The bar filled with smoke, and the bartender hit the floor. The five kids couldn't see much, but what they saw was the most anyone knew about it.

When the six-shooter clicked on empty, the bartender came up from behind with a 12 gauge shotgun and ordered them to get out and chased them into the street. Neither one had been hit, although the ends of the building had a lot of holes in them. The bartender chased them all away, including the kids. Dunsmore never came back, and Crandell was not allowed back in the bar unless he left his gun at home. This was the fight at the corral, and most were not in for it again—but the kids never forgot it.

This story appeared in the Jemez Thunder, *July 1, 1999.*

◀▶ THE MAN WHO TRAINED BURROS ◀▶

For several years, a man named Cox lived in a grove of trees between Cañon and Jemez Springs along the Jemez River. He had a corral there, and a campsite with a tent and an outside camp fire for cooking, and makeshift chairs and stumps to sit on to eat around his cooking pot. He dealt in burros, and my father knew him quite well.

He had trained four of them to work as a team and they pulled a ramshackle old buggy that wobbled along. The first time I saw him was when I was about 10 years old. He pulled into our corral with much whooping and hollering and plenty of cuss words. My brother and I were scared of this old man and his ragged clothes and his donkeys. We summoned our father, and he said, "Why, it's the burro tramp come to see us." From then on, the old hermit was called "the Burro Tramp." He stayed with us for a couple of days and he and his burros rested and ate hay, and Cox ate all the grub we had at the table. He left after he had bummed some meat and potatoes and some old pieces of harness he pieced for his four-burro team.

Sometime later, my father said "It's about noon. Let's visit old Cox at his camp." We stopped there, and the old man was delighted. He invited us for coffee, and got some bowls and spoons and invited us to dip into the stew that simmered in an old iron pot on the open fire. The stew tasted good, and Cox said to dip down in the bottom of the pot where "there are some chipmunks that I caught in my figure-four traps." We declined.

While there, he told my father about a dude that came up from Albuquerque to fish in his river and had a fancy car. Well, old Cox took the battery out and lugged it home and hooked it up to burn lights in his tent. When the fisherman came back, he couldn't start his car and there was no one to help, so he came to Cox's camp and explained his trouble. Cox went with him to see what his trouble was, and told him that someone had taken his battery. Cox said, "I have one in my tent. I'll sit in the dark, but I'll sell it to you for $20 just to get you started." He took the battery out and reinstalled it for free, then told the fisherman that he ought to have a dog to watch things while he was gone. He agreed to buy Cox's dog for $5. Cox had to get into the car and introduce him to the driver. Finally they drove off together, the dog and the fisherman. My father remarked it was one way to get money from town fishermen. Cox said, "I've traded this dog along the way to different people, and the dog always came back. That son of a gun kept my dog."

This story appeared in the Jemez Thunder, *October 15, 1999.*

A HIDEAWAY FOR THE WANTED

Some people have asked me if we had a place in the mountains to hide people who were wanted by state or federal law enforcement. A mysterious man who seemed to have unlimited wealth came here from Chicago, and began to build a place where wanted criminals could disappear until the heat was off. He had construction materials imported by the railroad to Porter Landing, then hauled up the canyon to several miles above the Seven Springs Fish Hatchery, where he had purchased a large piece of land. It was just before the new road was cut over Fenton Hill.

The materials were hauled up the canyon in freight wagons by Mack Fenton and a neighbor, Julian. The construction was new to us and imported à la "Death Valley Scotty." *[Ed. Note: Walter Edward Perry Scott, also known as Death Valley Scotty, was a prospector, performer, and con man made famous by his many scams involving gold mining in the early 20th century.]* They built a motel of sorts and a main meeting hall with a huge fireplace. They were ahead of our time, as they all had indoor plumbing and nice fixtures for running water, as well as electric lights. There were bunk houses, barns, and tack rooms. There was a dairy barn, a place for horses and rodeo grounds, all beautifully done. There was a pistol range and a skeet shoot and rifle range where the customers could get acquainted with their Tommy guns. The place was fenced, and a guard with a rifle let inside only those that were known.

As the building continued, a road was hacked out of La Cueva over Fenton Hill for cars. In the meantime, Seth Seiders, the man with unlimited funds, built a house above Hummingbird Lodge across the river. This place, called Rancho Chico, was a luxury place with gold faucets, fine furniture, and murals on the walls. This was for Seth Seiders's wife. The hideaway in the mountains was called Rancho Rea, the wife's name. Seth Seiders told me once that he had made a lot of money in the advertising business, as he was the first to use color, all the pictures in those days being black and white.

When the hideaway was run, it was staffed by people who had made their mark as rodeo riders. The foreman was Shorty Kelso, the Madison Square championship cowboy for 1927. We began to meet strangers on the road, with grim-faced drivers in Duesenbergs, Stutzes, Cadillacs and Pierce Arrows. They had hired a wild young cowboy to be the courier between Jemez Springs and Albuquerque. They called him Casey Jones, and he made the name fit. They bought him a new Model A pickup and scared us all. All the local people were afraid they might meet him on a little one-way road. We were invited once to a rodeo which had the best of riders, though a little fuzzy with drink. We saw Shorty Kelso bulldog a big steer from the running board of a 1927 Chevrolet Roadster— quite a feat, but there were some fine ladies from the East to cheer him on.

When I was about 10 years old, I brought a milk cow for their herd. Shorty put me up in the bunkhouse for the night. A poker game was going on for most of the night, and sometimes the guests would sit in. I don't think they did very well. The night I was there, a wrangler named Emmitt Smith from over on the Piñas Negras, won all the big pots.

The place ran until 1938, after the 18th Amendment (Prohibition) was repealed. Most of the bootleggers from the East, and most of the bank robbers on the most wanted list, were caught. A lot of things happened. Casey Jones rode his pickup into the Jemez River somewhere above Battleship Rock and came away with bruises. He and Rea had a thing going, and they went away together. We don't know how much it cost

Seth Seiders, but his wealth dried up and most of the horses and tack were sold. My sister still has a fine saddle marked SS, for Seth Seiders. The place was vacant a time and was finally sold as a dude ranch. The season was short, and it was hard to reach. One of several owners was the penitentiary warden at Santa Fe. Another owner was Ray Craig, who called the ranch The Lazy Ray. He was killed in Albuquerque. In 1970, the place was torn down and all traces were covered up. The hideaway was no more.

This story appeared in the Jemez Thunder, *November 1, 1999.*

◄►SHEEP CAMP◄►

Most flocks of sheep had about 1,000 sheep and a couple of herders, though some had even more and needed three or four herders. The supplies were a tent and a tin stove, a sack of beans, rice, salt and pepper, canned milk, and some chile. Any extra goodies were dependent on their sponsor. They were expected to eat mutton and try to use any of the crippled and those who could not keep up. There were three burros, a leader with a bell around her neck who carried the tent and the bedding, and the others carried the tin stove and groceries and salt for the sheep. These burros were trained to move ahead of the flock to a camping place for the night. These were usually used many times, and when the burros reached the old camping place, they laid down until someone could unload them. Of course, there were two dogs to help herd the sheep.

The grazing of the sheep started in the lower and warmer country, then moved to the high country for the summer and returned to warmer weather for the winter. During this trip, the sheep were marked with tar to show the owners. Sometimes they had to be dipped for ticks, which was called sheep dip and made of creosote. Each herd had a number of black sheep, usually one of every 50, so that the herders could count the black sheep and, if all were there, it meant none were lost. If a black sheep was missing, anywhere from one to 50 could be lost, though it usually proved to be 25 or less. The way you counted sheep was good for those who could not count beyond 10. The counter dug three small holes in the ground and gathered a handful of pebbles. His partner pushed the sheep through a corral or a hole in the fence, and when 10 went by, he placed a pebble in the first hole. When the hold held 10 pebbles, he took them out and put a pebble in the second hole (100 sheep). When he had 10 pebbles in the third hole, there were 1,000 sheep.

The burros stayed around the camp and sometimes they fed the lead burro, which was sort of a pet, usually white or spotted. When they loaded the burros to pick up salt (important), they loaded them with panniers, which are two boxes that hung on either side of the pack saddles. Each box would hold a 100-pound sack of salt.

They came to our ranch, as it was the farthest north near the Baca Location. The herders started them the 10 miles down the trail, and they eventually came to the ranch, where we let them in and took off their panniers. The herder came later and spent the night. The next day, he loaded the burros with 100 pounds of salt on each side, and started them up the trail for the camp, while the herder visited. If no one was there to unload them, they lay down to soften the weight. Not so dumb. The dogs were pretty smart themselves. If it happened that two herds were mixed, the dogs separated them by their scent.

The sheepherders were the most lonesome people in the world. If you stumbled onto a camp, they would invite you to a dinner of beans and mutton, with rice and raisins for dessert.

They would beg you not to leave to hear the news, and invite you back any time. It was imperative that you spoke Spanish.

This story appeared in the Jemez Thunder, *January 1, 2000.*

◀▶SOME TROUT FISH◀▶

Many years ago, my father traded for about 30 head of cows that were long of horn and a little wild. Steve Edsel had purchased a homestead on the Piñas Negras from a Hugh Bryan. The cattle were gone and Mr. Edsel traded for these steers to replenish his cattle business. He had some good fields of barley for winter feed.

My brother and I were to drive the cattle to Piñas Negras, a strange country for us to go to, but we started out. I was 11 and my brother was 13. These cattle were good travelers, but we found each time we crossed a river, half of them went down and half of them up the river. Each time we would round them up, and never lost any of them. When we got to Moon Canyon by way of Rancho Rea and the Fenton place, we were on the Calaveras and found the cows had mixed with a herd of 50 or more in Moon Canyon. It took a while to separate our cattle, but we were lucky as all our cows had long horns and were easy to identify.

We arrived at the Edsel ranch late in the evening and found the only one on the place was a man from old Mexico. He was living in the bunkhouse and doing his own cooking, which was bacon, hotcakes and beans. We did not understand him, and he did not bother to listen to a couple of kids. We were to stay there for two days and help this man sort things out.

The second day there we heard about Dove Creek, which had some trout. We rode our horses over the next ridge and unwound our hooks and line and cut willow poles to catch some small trout. When we came back that evening, we brought some nice small trout with us. My brother could cook trout, so he salted them and rolled them in cornmeal, then fried them in hot grease. They were very good! This giant of a man was very suspicious of fried trout, but he loved them. As we ate, we noticed that he pulled heads off and just ate them, bones and all! My brother and I knew he would soon choke to death, and we were really apprehensive.

Sure enough, on the third one he did choke, and went into a fit of coughing and choking. His chair turned over backwards, and he floundered on the floor. We abandoned the bunkhouse and went outside, as we knew he was dying and there was no place to get help. He finally rolled out on the porch, but we dared not touch him because of his convulsions, so we went back inside. We went to bed but lay awake wondering what to do about the dead man on the porch.

Who knows? About midnight he got up, came inside, and went to bed. We had hotcakes and syrup for breakfast, but the big man did not eat anything. By noon, he was well again, and we ate beans. We left the next day for the long ride home, but we never forgot this man who came near death because of some little trout!

This story appeared in the Jemez Thunder, *December 15, 2000.*

◄►THE JEMEZ BELL ◄►

This story begins when Francisco Coronado explored New Mexico in 1540. That year he wintered on top of the hill coming out of Bernalillo on what is now Highway 44. He looked up the Rio Grande and up the Jemez, and plans were made to colonize and convert all the Indians. Priests were brought in, and a church was built at each pueblo. Going up the river, there was Santa Ana, Zia, and Jemez. These churches were all built of adobe, and most still stand.

The last and furthest up the river was Jemez, where there was a small but energetic Indian tribe. This church was built out of rocks and was special. The story goes that a huge bell was cast and brought from Mexico City by ox cart to hang in the stone belfry. In the late 1600s, the Indians revolted because of the treatment by the Spaniards and the priests that ran the churches and the missions. The Indians expelled the Spanish out of New Mexico, killing some and burning their holdings. The Jemez Springs church was no exception, except it was more brutal than the rest. The Indians burned the church, and the two priests assigned there were taken out on the parade ground in front of the church. They were stripped of their robes and forced to crawl on their hands and knees while the Indians rode them around like burros, whipping them with cactus. Of course, they were soon dead.

The wrecked and pillaged church became a ruin, but no one knew where the bell went. Presumably it was hidden by some of the loyal converts. It took the Spaniards about 40 years to reconquer New Mexico. When they got to Jemez Springs, they spent a lot of time and effort looking for the bell. In retaliation for the torture of the priests, the Spaniards killed most of the men and enslaved the rest. The village was wiped out and ceased to exist.

Later came the homesteaders and ranchers, and the story of the bell was told and retold. Some said it weighed 1,000 lbs. and was rich in gold and silver, which had been added to the bronze casting to give it a special tone. Everyone hunted for the bell—including me! We thought it would make us rich if it were melted down or sold to a museum. How could the bell be moved without a wagon or cart, and while the riot was going on? Some of us thought the bell might weigh less than 500 lbs., comparing it with other church bells, and it might have weighed even half that much.

Of course, it was never found to this day.

In 1933, when the Civilian Conservation Corps (CCC) camps came to the Jemez Mountains, one of their projects was to stop or slow the deterioration of the old stone church in Jemez Springs and the nearby huts. The CCC boys mixed cement in wheelbarrows, and one can see the patches they made on top of the walls.

Harvey Barlow was a local man who was in charge of the project (and later a forest ranger and a friend of ours). I kidded him about using his crew to hunt for the bell, and he surprised me by saying he knew where it was! It seems that, as they dug around the foot of the belfry and the two little rooms beside it that held gear for the church, they discovered a tunnel that ran into a hillside towards the river. Some of the young men crawled down into the crumbling tunnel, although they were afraid of snakes or a cave-in. When Mr. Barlow saw what they were doing, he called them out and had the tunnel mouth filled with rock and dirt. He was convinced that the bell is in that escape tunnel, and I believe him. It would have been the quick and easy way to hide the bell during the riot. No one ever dug for it, even if they had known about the tunnel. Now, of course, it is forbidden.

We used to keep our horses in the ruin, as it was a great corral, and it took only a wood pole or two to keep them in. Transients used the old ruin for shelter.

This story appeared in the Jemez Thunder, *April 15, 1999.*

◄►LOST ON THE BACA RANCH◄►

In about 1938, three people were lost on the Baca Ranch. It was wintertime, and the snow was really bad that year. As clouds gathered and the snow came, three hunters went out on a chance to kill a deer and have something to eat for the winter. These were not mountain men and had no knowledge of this country. The rifle they carried had several cartridges and late in the evening they shot at a deer, but he was only crippled and ran away. They followed him to get another shot from the .30-30 rifle.

It started to snow, and they found themselves a few miles from their winter shacks. They finally stopped and looked around and realized that they were lost, and the deer was gone. There were three cartridges left in the rifle and only four matches carried by a 12-year-old boy. What to do? Nighttime in the woods could reach 40 degrees below zero, and only two of them had heavy jackets. In danger of freezing and nothing to eat, they finally managed to find a big tree that had fallen and decided to cuddle together to keep warm. With some pitch from the tree and a sheet of paper from a notebook, they managed to get a fire started, which left them with three matches for another night, if needed.

The next morning, it had quit snowing, but the snow was waist-deep and everything looked the same. They started out—and went the wrong way. They trekked all day and at night found a good place to build a fire with plenty of wood and some shelter from fallen trees. Now two matches left. They were really hungry by now and faced another night of bitter cold. Might as well have been lost in Alaska!

The day broke bright and clear, and by this time their relatives got in touch with the New Mexico Lumber and Timber Company, which sent out a search plane from Albuquerque. The plane was far off course, as the pilot was not familiar with the country. He did not see the lost hunters, although the hunters could see the plane. Now it looked bad for them again, but one of the old-timers remembered a solution: find a stream and follow it downhill and you will come to a road or a house—good advice for anyone lost in the woods.

The next day they waded waist-deep in the snow and came to a stream that was covered with ice and snow. They found a rock by the creek and broke through the ice and found that it flowed to the left. They followed the river all day, and by night they were very tired and found a place to stop and built another fire. They shot at a squirrel but missed, and now they were down to one cartridge and one match.

They had followed the San Antonio River from the Valle Grande, and the next day they pushed on and found a house a mile away that belonged to Glenn Barber, who was up cooking breakfast. He had heard about these fellows and was very surprised to see them at his door. Of course, they were very hungry, black from the fires and frost-bitten, but glad to be alive. Glenn immediately saddled a horse and went out to the highway while they ate. A big log truck came and picked them up. They were home again—with one match and one bullet for the gun!

This story appeared in the Jemez Thunder, *October 1, 2001.*

119

BAR HEART registered Routledge Ranch brand.

This drawing appeared in the Jemez Thunder, *July 1, 2000*

◄►ABOUT THE STORYTELLER◄►

Joe Routledge was the third generation of his family to live in New Mexico. His great aunt had come to Cañon in the Jemez Valley to teach school in 1883. His grandfather, William McCloskey, was a tinsmith who came to New Mexico Territory in 1888. He married Mabel Cornell, who was living with an aunt in Albuquerque. One of their children was Joe's mother, Ethel.

Joe lived with his family on the Freelove Canyon ranch until he was drafted at the start of World War II. He served as an infantryman in the South Pacific for two years and later privately published a collection of letters he wrote to his mother titled *64 Days on Okinawa.* Before going overseas, he married Mardell Spiker. After the war, they moved to Southern California where he lived until his death in 2014. They had three daughters: Sharon, Gail and Dodi. Described as one of those people who could "fix anything," he worked throughout his life as a mechanic and machinist.

Ethel and Art separated and subsequently divorced. Art died at age 51 of a heart attack. Ethel stayed in Albuquerque and went back to school. She attended the University of New Mexico at the same time as two of her children, and all received degrees. She remarried and lived to age 94.

◄►ABOUT THE EDITOR◄►

Judith Isaacs has lived in the Jemez Mountains since 1996 and served as director of the Jemez Springs Public Library from 1997-2015. She is an avid student of Southwest history and archaeology. Since retirement, she has volunteered as writer and editor for a website devoted to local history sponsored by the Jemez Springs Public Library (www.jemezvalleyhistory.org). She started her publishing company, Butterfly & Bear Press, before moving to New Mexico and has written and published three books about the Jemez Mountains: *Jemez Valley Cookbook: The Food, the People the Land; Guide to the Jemez Mountain Trail;* and *Into Hot Water.*

Made in the USA
Monee, IL
11 September 2023

42477411R00072